# STANDING
# OVATION
# PRESENTATIONS

*Discover Your Unique Communication Style & Let It Shine.*

# COPYRIGHT NOTICES

# CONTENTS

# ACKNOWLEDGMENTS

I am extremely happy to have this book out in the world so that I can share my passion for improving presentations with so many more people. I want to take this opportunity to acknowledge a few people who helped me turn the dream of writing a book into a reality. Even though I am an evangelist for encouraging more face-to- face communication, this book might not have come to fruition without a coincidental string of events involving social networking. I sent an email newsletter to one of my neighbors who sent it to another neighbor who happened to be a book agent and wondered why I didn't have a book listed in my bio. So I'd like to thank Gail Fox for passing along my email to Linda Konner who became my agent and has been invaluable in guiding me through this process. I'd also like to thank Motivational Press Publishing for working with me to make this book the best it could be.

A kiss and a hug to Nancy and Bob Steed of *Performance Plus* and Liz Laboy, Steve Burghardt, Willie Tolliver and Ed Laboy of *Leadership Transformation Group* who have given me such incredible experiences and opportunities and taught me so much about training. I would like to thank my mother, Elena Verzieri, for raising me to believe that I can accomplish anything. Huge appreciation goes out to my husband Ken Becker for supporting me while I pursued the careers and opportunities that helped me to develop the material shared in this book and who was one of the first people to painstakingly read the completed manuscript. I can truthfully say I could not have done any of this without Ken. And speaking of painstaking reading, I want to give a huge thanks and a shout out to Michele LaRue for doing such a thorough editing job of this manuscript under very challenging conditions. Thanks also goes out to my incredible posse of friends; Amy Ferris, who in addition to being incredibly generous and supportive, asked me to write for *Dancing at the Shame Prom* (Seal Press, 2012) which gave me my first published author credit. A big thank you, also, to Joyce, Claire and Laurie for supporting and listening to me throughout this process. Thanks to *Savor the Success* and *Ladies Who Launch*, two women's networking organizations that have helped encourage, inform and support me during this process. And I somehow wouldn't feel complete without acknowledging my son, Nolan Becker, for being all that he is, making me so proud and forcing me to learn about the world of sports which is so ripe for metaphor. And thanks to all of the wonderful companies and individuals who I have had the pleasure of training, coaching and presenting to. You have all taught me a tremendous amount and I am grateful to all of you. I hope you all continue to work on elevating the way you communicate. I continue to be here to help.

# PREFACE

## WHY DO STARS SHINE?

"A star shines because nuclear fusion (the process by which multiple atomic particles join together to form a heavier nucleus) releases energy which traverses the star's interior and then radiates into outer space."

In other words, a lot of small particles get together in the middle of the star and work to their full potential. Those little particles work so hard that they create enough energy to make that star shine brightly enough for us to see it billions of miles away.

But what about the multiple particles that make up your core? What are they and how hard are they working? Can your energy be seen from miles away?

We all possess a wealth of incredible qualities – our particles. Some of them we were born with, some of them we've accumulated through our own experiences. When we identify, own, and put all these incredible qualities or particles to work, we begin to shine.

This book will help you discover your unique "particles" and teach you how to put them to work in order to radiate enough energy to shine for miles!

I've brought together my varied experiences collected from years of professional acting, TV, and film writing; teaching and training; motherhood and community service to create this energized contribution to the world of communication training. I hope you enjoy it.

# ABOUT THIS BOOK

Research proves that over 90% of communication is nonverbal. Nevertheless, we all – business executives, political leaders, job seekers, and other professionals – continue to place more emphasis on *what* we are saying rather than on *how* we are saying it. With our growing dependence on *virtual* communication, effective *face-to-face* communication is becoming a lost art. I believe that meaningful and successful relationships can only be developed through meaningful and successful communication. This book aims to educate readers as to the importance of face-to-face communication, while giving them specific techniques to make all aspects of their face-to-face communication more authentic and engaging.

With more highly qualified individuals vying for fewer positions, it is more important than ever for all of us to discover how best to stand out. This book offers easy-to-implement tips and advice, presented in an entertaining way that will give you the tools and skills to outshine your competition – whether on a job interview, at a party, or on the job.

*Standing Ovations Presentations* will introduce you to *ActorTyping* – a concept I developed. Famous celebrities have specific qualities and characteristics that make them shine. I have identified nine well-known actor *types* by these qualities and characteristics. I believe we all have similar qualities and can use these qualities to stand out and become stars in our own right. I will share examples and anecdotes based on Hollywood celebrities and on my experiences with clients; Dos and Don'ts for each *ActorType* are explained and are provided.

In addition to *ActorTyping*, *Standing Ovations Presentations!* provides clear, concrete, practical advice on how to improve the three Vs of effective communication: the **Visual, Vocal, and Verbal** skills. Each communication skill has its own chapter, in which I detail its value and impact. I share with you all of the creative training exercises I've been using for years with my clients and students to help you polish each individual skill. And occasionally, I will get up on my "Soapbox" and rant about a pet peeve of mine.

An important concept that sets this book apart from other books on the topic is my introduction of the Fourth "V" of effective communication: **Value.** The consistency between how one appears and what one values is what helps turn an ordinary actor into a star – and an ordinary person into a superstar communicator. Throughout the book I will guide you on uncovering the values that you presently hold and teach you how to align them with your communication style.

If you faithfully and courageously follow through on the exercises and tips I have laid out, you will begin to polish your strengths so that they radiate and shine like they never have before.

# FROM SHY TO SHY-NING

*Experience is not what happens to a man; it is what a man does with what happens to him." ALDOUS HUXLEY*

I've been a professional actress for over 20 years and a public speaking coach for more than 15. I've performed live in front of hundreds of people, and spoken and presented in front of many large crowds – which is amazing, considering I didn't speak intelligibly until I was nearly three years old. And when I did begin to speak, getting a full sentence out of me was like pulling teeth. I was so painfully shy that at a family gathering at which I cowered behind my mother as usual, one of my uncles addressed me as "Shy" – everyone laughed and just like that a nickname was born. My nickname stuck – for 12 years!! My real name was ignored and neglected; in its place was "Shy." I was addressed as "Shy," referred to as "Shy," introduced as "Shy." Even on the family Christmas cards my mother wrote "Shai." (The fancy spelling didn't obliterate the meaning, but it did cause people to wonder whether I was adopted from China.)

Scientists now posit that traits like shyness can be genetic. I recently conducted a survey where over 60% of the respondents admitted to being or having been shy. Although some respondents attributed their shyness to the fact that one of their parents was also shy, most respondents could trace their shyness to a situation or a set of circumstances. I'm not sure if my shyness was the result of an inherited "shy gene" or if my shyness was the result of having been born into an extremely talkative family and not having the energy or wherewithal to speak out. All I can remember about that period of my life is the feeling of wanting to disappear the moment anyone turned their attention towards me.

So, how did I get from "Shai" to where I am today? I made a very deliberate choice. Somehow I knew that I did not want to continue being type cast as the shy background player in the movie of my life. I yearned to step out of that role. It was suffocating me but I didn't feel capable of being anyone else. Shai was familiar, she was comfortable, she was well liked – respected even – but she was driving me crazy! If you are reading this book, chances are there is a quality or habit that you feel locked into but would like to release. That's just how I felt. So, I made a choice.

The deliberate choice I made to step out of my shyness wasn't premeditated, but as soon as I made it, I knew it was right. It was my freshman year in a new high school. A new PUBLIC high school – I had gone to Catholic school up till then. I was sitting in homeroom class listening to the daily announcement over the loud speaker. At the tail end of the vice principal's litany of information, she announced auditions for a new play that was going to be put on at the boy's school down the street. It was as if fate had whispered in my ear, tapped me on the shoulder, and hit me on the head all at the same time. Without thinking or rationalizing it away, I took down the information. My mother had tried getting me out of my shyness before by enrolling me in acting classes at a neighborhood playhouse. It hadn't worked. In fact, I remember very little about the experience. Maybe because it had been her idea, or maybe because it traumatized me. However, I suppose the idea that acting might be my ticket out of the Shy prison remained with me.

The second-most-important decision I made once I decided to audition for this play, was not to tell anyone about my plan. I somehow instinctively knew that the wrong response from my family (or the one friend I had at the time) would increase the chance of my not following through. How many times have you shared a dream, desire, or goal before you should have and allowed yourself to be talked out of it?

To audition for the school play I needed a two-minute monologue. But I had no idea where I could find a two-minute monologue suitable for a shy, 14-year-old African-American girl. I searched the school library but came up short – so I wrote my own. It was an extremely melodramatic rant about being dumped by a boyfriend I'd never even had.

After I wrote my monologue and counted down the days to the audition, it was as if the tiny particles – the ones I was born with and the ones I had developed during my grade school years – had fused together to create the energy that catapulted me into that school auditorium on the afternoon of the auditions. Suddenly there was Shai standing in front of complete strangers, revealing raw emotions that she had written about herself.

A skill I often use in my teaching and coaching is based on an acting technique called substitution: if you haven't lived an experience, you think of an experience that brings out similar emotions in order to make the performance believable. During that high school audition, when I let out the anger, disappointment, frustration, and rage towards this imaginary boyfriend, I was actually using the anger, disappointment, frustration, and rage that had been trapped inside of "Shai" all those years. All the qualities and strengths I had been hiding for years … suddenly had free rein.

After what I am sure were two minutes of complete overacting, the director sat me down. He studied me as though he wasn't quite sure what to make of me. He wanted to know where I got the monologue. When I told him I'd written it, he wanted to know if I'd ever been dumped. He asked me all sorts of other questions and apparently liked the answers that I gave him, because I was cast as the Sphinx in Jacques Cocteaux's *The Infernal Machine*. It was a fantastic role. A role with which I had to be powerful, strong, respected, and intimidating. A very far cry from the "Shai" everyone knew, I adored performing the part and got terrific feedback and the rest, as they say, is history…

Because of my intimate knowledge of being shy and knowing what it's like to feel unable to grab the spotlight, I have become extremely passionate about empowering others to uncover and unleash their inner "Star power." What people need to understand is that they don't have to become actors, or even professional public speakers, to allow themselves to be more powerful communicators. Good communication techniques will make you a better boss, colleague, partner, parent, friend, and individual.

It may not happen all at once. A few weeks of playing the Sphinx did not turn me into a chatterbox, but it definitely added some very important qualities, or particles, to my inner core – particles that I utilized as I gradually went from being a shy background player in the movie of my life to a strong supporting actor and then to the leading lady I feel I am today.

In looking back over my journey, I can't help but wonder ... if I had talked myself out of that one audition, might another opportunity have presented itself? Probably. Would I have acted on that one? Possibly. I believe opportunities present themselves to us daily. It takes courage and trust to act on them. How many opportunities to shine have you passed up? The fact that you are reading this book shows that you are ready to take a step towards rewriting the script of your life.

# SETTING THE STAGE – RESEARCH, STATISTICS, AND METHODOLOGY

Red-carpet shows that precede major award ceremonies have become almost more popular than the award shows themselves. Viewers are glued to their screens to see if their favorite star is shining, fading, or self-imploding on the red carpet. A major percentage of tabloid content is taken up with photographs that depict what a particular celebrity wore, how much he weighs, what she's done with her hair, how close he or she is standing to their significant other, and so on.

I once asked a fitness expert, who was on the staff of a major women's fitness magazine, why the magazine never put "real" models on their covers. I wanted to know why they always choose skinny, sexy actresses in two-piece bathing suits to grace the front page. She told me she'd argued the same point with her colleagues but was told that studies proved the magazine sold better with reed-thin movie stars on the cover. This turns out to be true for most magazines. Market research study after market research study shows that women, especially, will be more likely to buy a magazine if the model on the cover is young, thin, and beautiful. The more recognizable and attractive the celebrity, the better the sales. This is true for fitness magazines, news magazines, and, of course, tabloids. Does this fact that we are obsessed with physical attractiveness reflect the shallowness of our current society? Not necessarily. Read on and I'll explain why.

A renowned professor from UCLA, named Albert Mehrabian, conducted a famous study on communication back in the seventies. His study focused on how three different elements contributed to the effectiveness of an individual's ability to communicate emotion. He called these three different elements the three Vs of effective communication and, after extensive research, he assigned a percentage to the role each element played in the effectiveness of communication. Here are the Three Vs. Before you turn the page, rank these three elements according to what you think is their order of importance. Put a "1" next to the element you think is most important and a "3" next to the one you think least important.

## THE 3 VS OF EFFECTIVE COMMUNICATION

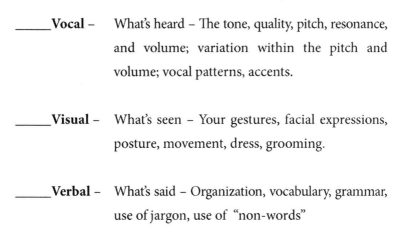

_____**Vocal** – What's heard – The tone, quality, pitch, resonance, and volume; variation within the pitch and volume; vocal patterns, accents.

_____**Visual** – What's seen – Your gestures, facial expressions, posture, movement, dress, grooming.

_____**Verbal** – What's said – Organization, vocabulary, grammar, use of jargon, use of "non-words"

Picking up on my cues from the beginning of this chapter, many of you may have ranked the Visual element as the most important. But what did you rank second in importance? Professor Mehrabian's research netted these results:

**Visual** impacts **55%** of the message; **Vocal 38%** and **Verbal 7%**

It's important to understand that these statistics are not meant to imply that what you say is not important. What is important to understand is that listeners will be more affected by how you look, what you do, and how you sound, and less affected by the actual words coming out of your mouth. Ralph Waldo Emerson said it best, way before Dr. Mehrabian conducted his research.

*"What you do speaks so loud, I can not hear what you say."*

How brilliant is that! And how true. When we think we are communicating, we are often doing something that is distracting our listeners from being able to hear what we are actually saying.

In order for you to seem believable, confident, organized, and likeable, you need to *look* and *sound* believable, confident, organized, and likeable. Your Three Vs need to be consistent. If how you look and how you sound is boring or lacking in confidence, then no matter what you say, your listeners will get the feeling that you are boring and lacking in confidence. And the reverse is true as well. How many of you have been in situations where two people have said almost exactly the same thing, but one person is ignored while the other is lauded for being a genius? Moreover, how many of you have been the one being ignored? If you continue reading this book and faithfully follow the exercises that follow, I can promise you that this will not happen again.

Professor Mehrabian's experiment has been repeated, challenged, and argued over again and again. Many people assert that the research on the Three Vs of Communication was based solely on the impact of emotional communication. However, other research supports the fact that if we want to engage, persuade, or convince someone of something, it is important to connect with them on an emotional level. Therefore, even if the statistics arrived at by Dr. Mehrabian apply only to emotional communication, they hold true for the majority of communication that we conduct on a daily basis – because on a daily basis we have a need to engage, persuade, and convince our listeners.

Other research has been done since Professor Mehrabian's study and that research still indicates that our nonverbal communication accounts for 60 – 80% of our overall communication.

The actual numeric statistics vary, but not hugely. Some people say it takes 30 seconds to form an opinion that could last a lifetime, while some say it takes 7 – 17 seconds to form an opinion. An article in the May 29, 2000, *New Yorker* reports on a demonstration by social psychologists. This shows that we need only about 10 – 15 seconds of videotape to form a lasting impression about another person. In the book *Blink*, Malcolm Gladwell talks about how humans have the ability to instinctually "know" something about a person, an object, or a situation in just 2 seconds. Personally, I'm with him. In this age of shortened attention spans, it takes 2-3 seconds to make a first impression.

In *Blink*, Gladwell writes about how the visual impression not only affects our impression of a person, place, or thing but also subconsciously affects the decisions and choices that we make. He writes about an experiment showing that the way musicians looked during their orchestra auditions impacted the way they were perceived and whether they subsequently were hired. This bias was finally dealt with by having orchestras implement blind auditions – auditioning the musician from behind a screen. Unfortunately for most of us who are called upon to give a presentation or a speech, standing behind a screen is not an option.

Why would an orchestra director care whether or not a musician looked a certain way? Did the director consciously decide that they wanted their orchestra members to look a certain way? Probably not; it was most likely a subconscious choice.

*"New research being done by psychologist Nancy Etcoff shows that when human beings see an attractive person the reward centers in the brain fire. [… ]As Psychologist John R. Buri has shown, initial attraction to a person is just a powerful wave of neurotransmitters sent our way. This essentially creates a brain flooding of many different rewards, including Epinephrine, Dopamine, Phenyl ethylamine and Endorphins. Such powerful rewards for such surface level beauty can*

*suggest many things, including an explanation for the commonly held belief that attractive people are more successful in life."* "How The Brain Reacts To Attractiveness," Psychology in the News, May 3, 2010

How many of you are thinking, "So what if it's supported by research? The research just proves that human beings are a bunch of superficial, judgmental snobs." I hear you, but that's not entirely the case. Though I won't argue the fact that we may be a nation overly focused on superficialities, I will argue that it's not entirely our fault. Judging strangers, and even people we know, by what we see doesn't mean that we're a species of snobs; it means we're a species with a strong desire to survive. Our tendency to judge people by what we see first, what we hear second, and what we say third, can be traced to our need for survival and safety.

**Blame It on Our Lizard Brain**

Many aspects of the human brain have evolved and are continuing to evolve. However, our mechanism for judging our surroundings visually first and auditorially second has not evolved very much over time. Our minds are still affected by our primitive First Brain: the instinctual and emotionally powerful limbic system and brain stem. Some scientist call this our Lizard or Monkey Brain. The First Brain works on the unconscious level – on instinct. The visual input from our eyes goes right to the First Brain "(First impression.)"

**All sensory input – sight, sound, touch, taste, and smell – is received by the First Brain where it is interpreted and sent to the Rational Brain.**

In other words the mechanism that causes us to assess whether Lindsay Lohan is on or off the wagon based solely on a tabloid photo is the same mechanism that kicked in thousands of years ago when we caught sight of a wildebeest while we were foraging for food. If our ancestors did not have the ability to quickly discern the difference between a hungry predator and a possible food source, they would have had a slim chance of survival.

So let's think of that ancestor of ours – he or she is foraging for food and sees a saber-toothed tiger. By seeing how far away the animal is, how hungry it looks, how large it is, and how strong it is, our ancestor instantly knows to flee, freeze, hide, or say a small prayer. Another one of our ancestors is a little farther away, but hears something that sounds like the roar of a lion. Judging by the sound of that roar, how far away it is, how strong it is, whether the lion sounds hungry, or whether the lion sounds hurt, that ancestor will have to quickly decide what direction he or she will continue in. In both those instances, our ancestors used the Visual and Vocal elements of communication to make a a critical life-or-death decision. That instinct is still alive and well in all of us today. Because of the way the brain is wired, that instinct loves to do its job and is, in fact, very good at it. And it's a stealth worker, which means it's doing its job without our even knowing it.

Here's another way I like to think of it: Imagine you and your message are hopeful guests at an exclusive red-carpet event. In order to be allowed in, you have to get through the bouncers positioned outside of the event. As we all know, bouncers first assess how you look. If your visual meets their criteria, then you're usually allowed in without having to even open your mouth.

Our First Brain works much like a bouncer. It "accepts" a person based on what it sees first. Pushing this analogy a bit further, if you don't look like you belong at the event, but tell the bouncer you're related to the guest of honor, the bouncer will then assess how convincing/believable you are in saying that. Did you stutter as you said it? Look down and use an anxious tone? Is your accent completely different from the accent of the guest of honor?

So, here you are, standing in front of the event, not looking like you belong ... and you don't sound like you're telling the truth. You will most likely remain on the outside, looking in. But what if you produce an authentic pass or happen to know the verbal secret password? Then the bouncer is forced to adjust his first impression of you and begrudgingly let you in.

A similar process happens during communication. Your listener assesses your visual and vocal cues and then once you open your mouth, employs the **Rational Brain** to confirm or adjust his or her first impression. But think of how much time this process could take. You're standing outside in the cold while other people are let in easily. And let's be honest: Sometimes, even though you've said the secret password, the bouncers probably still won't trust you completely and will most likely keep an eye on you the whole night. Or worse yet, they may dismiss your use of the password as a lucky guess and still not let you in. Comparatively, how many times have you experienced using the most thoughtful, logical, reasonable, understandable, intelligent words you can think of to explain something to someone and they still don't seem to hear, believe, or understand you? That person's "bouncers" may have already made their decision.

In an article in *The New Yorker*, ["Words on Trial", July 23, 2012] Jack Hitt writes, "[...] words serve as catalysts, setting off sparks of potential meaning that the listener organizes into more specific meaning by observing facial expressions, body language, and other redundant cues. We then employ another powerful tool: prior experience and the storehouse of narratives that each of us carries – what linguists call 'schema.' To every exchange we bring unconscious scripts; as any given sentence unspools, we readjust the schema to make better sense of what we are hearing." In other words, not only does our communication need to get through the physical non-verbal bouncers, our communication also needs to get through our listeners' preconceived unconscious scripts that are written by their past experience.

**Try This:**

Walk onto a bus or subway and look around at the strangers in front of you. How long does it take your unconscious brain to come up with a feeling or impression about the person you are looking at? Now based on that impression, think about whether you would or would not want to do business with that person, go to a party with that person, go on a date with him or her. What did you base that opinion or impression on? Now ask yourself what that person could do to change the opinion you've formed.

Many people delude themselves into thinking that "once they get to know me they'll see how _____ I am. So it doesn't really matter what I look or sound like." For those of you who feel that way, consider this:

**It takes people three times as long to change their opinion of you as it takes for them to form it. AND it can take between three and 12 visits to UNDO a negative first impression.**

Can you count on people giving you 12 opportunities to impress them?

Once a negative impression has been made on the First Brain, the advanced Rational Brain has to work much harder to take in and reinterpret the subsequent information being received. Sometimes our Rational Brain is a little slow in making its adjustment.

We can complain all we want about the "bouncers" outside an event but most of the time they are pretty intimidating and it's not usually a good idea to get into a fight with them. And when you think about it, their purpose is primarily not to judge you or keep you out, but to protect the people inside. The same is true of our "old" brain's bouncers. They are there to protect us. So instead of fighting other people's tendencies to perceive us incorrectly, why not create a perception which is difficult to misinterpret?

Please note: I am not suggesting that if you do X then everyone will LIKE you. That's impossible. Being liked and being perceived as authentic and congruent are two different things. The best we can hope for is to be consistent, clear, and effective, so that we increase the chances of our presence and our communication being allowed in. If our authentic, congruent self is communicated – "allowed in" – we've done our best. It's up to the other person to decide, based on their "schema," whether they like us or not.

**Knowing Is Growing**

You may be thinking that this judging people by the way they look is so unfair. To which I could give you the classic parent answer: **"Who said life is fair?"** But I won't do that.

The way I respond to these scientific statistics and the main reason I'm writing this book is because I believe "Knowledge is power." Since we **know** what people's brains instinctively do when they first meet us or interact with us, we have the **power** to adjust what they see.

**I am not suggesting that you run out and hire a plastic surgeon. There are so many other factors besides our physical features that go into our visual impression.**

While it's important to be visually engaging and visually effective, being engaging and effective does not always require you to be visually attractive. I will not lie and say that physical attractiveness is not a factor in the way we are perceived; abundant research proves that it is, but there is so much more to being attractive. Since the limbic brain of your listener is visually searching your physical appearance to assess how safe it is to interact with you, physical attractiveness is only part of what is being seen and only part of the criteria the listener uses to form their impression.

The way you stand, gesture, smile, use eyecontact, and utilize the tone of your voice can communicate immeasurable levels of attractiveness and engagement.

This book will teach you exactly how to harness the power of becoming visually engaging without ever going under a plastic surgeon's knife.

## The Unsung Fourth "V"

Traditional presentation books and many communication trainers emphasize the Three Vs from Professor Mehrabian's research that I've outlined above – The Visual, Vocal, and Verbal elements of communication. I've added a fourth "V." It stands for VALUE.

For me, in order to communicate fully and effectively, it is extremely important to know what Value I am bringing to the table and what Values I embody and live by. Remember our bouncer? He lets people in based on visual information that "fits his criteria." Similarly, everyone we meet carries around his or her own set of criteria based on their culture and previous experiences. The way you visually appear to one person may align with criteria they have set up for a trustworthy, interesting, powerful individual. However, according to another person's criteria, you may seem condescending, full of yourself, and manipulative. There is not always a lot you can do if someone misreads your message based on the fact that they do not share the same criteria.

However, the surest way to get through most people's preconceived criteria is to make sure the Visual, Vocal, and Verbal elements are consistent and congruent with what you truly value and what value you have to offer.

When your Visual, Vocal, and Verbal messages reflect your **Values** and communicate what **Value** you bring to your listener, you are going to look and sound more authentic and confident, and your presentation will be more likely to have a strong and positive impact. This is what is meant by the expression "play to your strengths." That expression is used a lot in the acting world. Playing to your strengths means making sure that everything you do, say, and stand for is aligned with your strengths and/or your values. Playing to your strengths also means finding out what you are excellent at – what makes you shine – and integrating that with your physical, mental, and spiritual self so that it all works for you and not against you.

I feel that in order to create a truly helpful book on communication and presentation skills, it is important for me to spend some time helping you discover your values and strengths. Knowing what your core values and strengths are will help you in identifying your ActorType and will allow you to be "cast" in roles that are not only comfortable and enjoyable for you but will also be engaging and enjoyable for your listeners and audiences.

# TYPE CASTING

Imagine Clark Gable starring in *The Babe Ruth Story* or Kathy Griffith as Scarlett in *Gone with the Wind*. Clark Gable's strength is not in his roughness or his "everyman" quality. Similarly, Kathy Griffith's strength is not her delicate beauty, gentile nature, or steely resolve. With all the makeup and wardrobe and acting coaching in the world, it would be difficult for those two people to authentically communicate the values and strengths of those two screen characters. It would be inconsistent with who they are and it would not seem authentic or believable. In the acting world when an actor plays someone who does not physically or psychically resemble them it is called – "playing against type."

One dictionary definition of **Type:**
1. a group made up of individuals or items that have strongly marked and readily defined similarities
2. somebody or something regarded as belonging to a group or category by virtue of having the main qualities associated with it
3. a person regarded as having a particular temperament or characteristics

The idea of "type" was instilled in me both in my career as an actor and as a writer for daytime dramas. As an actress, roles I was being called to audition for were categorized by type. An agent or casting director would decide (sometimes just based on a photo) whether or not I was the right type to even go in for the audition. Did the role call for a commercial type, a dramatic type, a young mom, girl next door, urban professional, street, hip, comedic, educated, uneducated, model, uptight business professional, sexy with a sense of humor, sexy with a sense of danger, and on and on. If I wasn't the right type, there was often no hope of being seen.

As a writer, I had to be acutely aware of the character types I wrote for. If you take a look at any soap opera, you will see all of the common Archetypes faithfully adhering to their common archetypical behavior and communicating in recognizable archetypical style. If I wrote the wrong line for the wrong type, the editor would have to cut it out or change it.

But typing is not relegated to the realm of entertainment. We categorize or type people on a daily basis. "He's such a _____ type, he wouldn't be interested in that." We categorize ourselves: "That's pretty but it's not the type of thing I would wear." We often use typing of ourselves and others to limit or explain behavior. I use typing as a way to understand and to make the most of our innate qualities and behavior.

## Why all the Type?

Everyone admires actors like Meryl Streep and Sean Penn for their versatility. They have the rare gift and fortune to be able to portray many different roles and span many types. However, most actors are best known for portraying variations on *one* type. In fact, most careers are made because an actor brands him-or herself as a specific type – Lucille Ball, Sylvester Stallone, Adam Sandler. In the acting world, always getting hired to play similar roles or characters is called being type cast. And as I mentioned above, casting Charlize Theron, who is known for her beauty and sex appeal, as the unattractive, unsympathetic serial killer she played in *Monster* is called "casting against type." Some actors are terrific at "playing against type," while others stretch our imaginations too much and fall flat. Interestingly, the actors who have the most trouble playing against type are those whose strengths are the most clearly defined.

During my many years of acting, I repeatedly heard actors say things like: "I don't want to typecast myself, I can play any role." And they would complain bitterly about not being able to audition for a particular role that was deemed not right for them. In my early years, I felt the same way. But the more I watched my fellow actors (both working and nonworking), the more I realized that we inherit, develop, and embody certain qualities that are unique to us. As actors, those qualities push us toward certain types and make us more believable and castable as those types. Fighting against those qualities takes a lot of energy and is rarely successful – unless, of course, you're Meryl Streep.

As a presentation skills coach, I've come to realize that nonactors fall into types as well. Our "type" is our way of expressing the values or character strengths that we inherently embody or have developed over the course of a lifetime. Most of us have what I refer to as a "default" type – the type we rely on the majority of the time. That type is either developed through experiences that occurred early on in life or is influenced by our collective unconscious as Caroline Myss suggests in her many books on Archetypes. The important thing to recognize is that we all exhibit behaviors which are unique to us and yet fall within parameters of certain universal types.

Based on my 30-plus years in the entertainment world, I have created my own personality typing system that is fun, accurate, and accessible – I call it The ActorType. Below is a list of the nine different ActorTypes. Most people are decidedly One type or are a combination of several types. In the next chapter I will explain the various ActorTypes in detail, identify the mythological/ psychological Archetypes they correlate with, list the values that drive them, point out the advantages and challenges for each type, and give you easy-to-implement tips on how to shine no matter what type you are.

## THE NINE ACTORTYPES

1. Hero/Heroine
2. Ingénue/ Innocent
3. Villain
4. Comic
5. Whiz Kid /Know-It-All
6. Super Hero/Action Hero

7. Super Model/Sex Symbol

8. Buddy

9. Salty Veteran/Curmudgeon

Social scientists, psychologists, and self-help experts have created many different assessment tools to codify people's values, character strengths, and personality types. My ActorType method expands upon, incorporates, and is informed by some of these tools. Three character assessment methods I will reference in describing the different ActorTypes are: VIACharacter, the DiSC profile, and Archetypes. So before we delve into the ActorTypes, I'd like to briefly explain these tools.

## VALUES IN ACTION (VIA)

In researching values for this book, I came across the relatively new field of positive psychology called Values in Action. http://www.viacharacter.org One of the founders of this field, Martin Seligman, and others identify 24 Values that represent a person's core character strengths. There are many other lists of values but what I like about Values in Action is that they concentrate not on values that we aspire to but on values that we act upon every day.

*"If you want to develop character, you have to identify your strengths and use them over and over again."* CHRIS PETERSON, *VIA* SCIENCE DIRECTOR.

*THE VIA TWENTY-FOUR VALUES ARE:*

1. Creativity: New ways of thinking and acting.
2. Curiosity: Exploring and seeking for its own sake.
3. Open-mindedness: Seeing things objectively and fairly, from all sides.
4. Love of learning: Constantly developing skills and knowledge.
5. Perspective: Seeing in ways that make sense and giving wise counsel.
6. Bravery: Not shrinking from threat, challenge, difficulty, or pain; acting on convictions even if unpopular.
7. Persistence: Seeing things through, despite difficulties.
8. Integrity: Presenting oneself in a genuine way; taking responsibility for one's feelings and actions.
9. Vitality: A zest and enthusiasm for life and living.
10. Love: Valuing, sharing, and caring for others.
11. Kindness: Doing things for others without requiring reciprocation.
12. Social intelligence: Being aware of how yourself and others are motivated, and acting accordingly.
13. Citizenship: Being socially responsible and loyal.
14. Fairness: Treating everyone in a similar way. Being just and without bias.
15. Leadership: Driving achievement whilst maintaining harmony.
16. Forgiveness and mercy: Forgiving wrongdoers rather than seeking punishment or revenge.

17. Humility/Modesty: Not putting oneself above others. Letting achievements speak for themselves.

18. Prudence: Not taking undue risks or doing what you will regret.

19. Self-regulation: Controlling one's emotions and actions according to one's values.

20. Wonder: Appreciating beauty and excellence.

21. Gratitude: Knowing, feeling, and being thankful for all the good things in life.

22. Hope: Positively expecting the best and working to achieve it.

23. Humor: Enjoying laughter and making people laugh. Seeing the lighter side of life.

24. Spirituality: Having coherent beliefs in a higher purpose and the meaning of life.

You can go to the VIA website, http://www.viacharacter.org and take their value survey and determine your top five character strengths. As I breakdown the nine ActorTypes, I will list several values that might be typical of each type. Knowing what your VIA Character strengths may help you identify ActorType.

## DiSC Assessment

The DiSC Profile instrument was developed by industrial psychologists over a 20-year period to measure how different people approach problem solving. It has grown to be a highly respected workplace assessment tool used in many corporate and business environments. DiSC is used to assess an individual's different communication styles, problem-solving skills, motivational triggers, stressors, and other behavioral styles. It's a wonderful workplace tool. By answering several questions online you receive an amazingly detailed 20+ page assessment. The four basic DiSC styles are listed below.

**D-Style (Dominance):** Succeeding is the motivation for D-Style people. They take action and achieve results instantly. D-Styles are strong-willed, forceful and determined. Their ultimate goal is independence.

**i-Style (Influence):** i-Styles are motivated by their interpersonal relationships. They enjoy collaboration and are considered to be enthusiastic, trusting, and impulsive. Mainly, their goal is to be desired.

**S-Style (Steadiness):** These people want to maintain stability. While they are calm, patient, and consistent, they fear change and value security. Their goals are accomplishing success and being accepted for their accomplishments.

**C-Style (Conscientiousness):** C-Style people are careful and systematic. Because their goal is accomplishment, they have a fear of being criticized. They are perfectionists who are motivated by gaining knowledge and showing their proficiency.

*(I am an authorized Inscape Exchange distributer – the number-one distributor for DiSC Profile assessments. If you would like to have an online DiSC profile assessment, contact me at Robyn@SpeakEtc. com. )*

For those of you who have already taken the DiSC assessment, I have included which DiSC profile(s) is/are most likely to be associated with each ActorType.

## ARCHETYPES

In addition to the various personality assessment tools I referenced to create my ActorTypes, there is the psychological and mythical concept of the Archetype. Joseph Campbell, Carolyn Myss, J. R. R. Tolkein, Peter Jackson, and the authors of fairy tales and myths utilize, talk about, and rely on the concept of Archetypes. But what are Archetypes?

## ARCHETYPES IN A NUTSHELL: (SKIP THIS IF YOU'VE EVER USED THE TERM "PSYCHO-BABBLE")

Carl Jung, one of the fathers of psychoanalysis, brought the word Archetype into everyday vernacular. Jung, most famous for his introduction of the Collective Unconscious to the field of psychoanalytic study, believed humans have two different levels of the unconscious: the personal unconscious and the collective unconscious. The personal unconscious contains all the information that has accumulated in a person's lifetime. The collective unconscious does not develop over the course of a person's life but is inborn and contains information that is shared by all human beings. Its language is the language of Archetypes. This further supports our Brain as Bouncer theory. Our First Brain makes its first impression based on what it knows about the Archetype from the depths of its collective unconscious, and our Rational Brain interprets the first impression from the experience of its personal unconscious.

In the years since Jung put forward his ideas about the Archetypes and the collective unconscious, the study and use of Archetypes has exploded. Carolyn Myss defines an Archetype as predefined patterns of behavior that each of us is born with. In her book *Sacred Contracts*, she explains how defining your Archetype can help guide you towards fulfilling the life you were meant to lead. Joseph Campbell has written several books for screenwriters about how Archetypes and myth are the backbone of story.

Whether you believe there is a collective unconscious or not, it's hard to ignore the fact that in all cultures and religions certain myths and fairytale figures emerge over and over again. If you look at the landscape of Hollywood, it's impossible to ignore the fact that actors and the roles they play fall into distinctly universal and identifiable types. It's also fascinating to discover how each one of us in our everyday lives has universal identifiable character traits.

I first developed my passion for and expertise in public speaking while teaching English to adult non-English-speaking learners. Teaching English as a second language taught me two important facts:

1) Communication has very little to do with language. I discovered this well before I heard of Dr. Mehrabian's study.

2) The same basic personality types appear in almost every culture. Whether I was teaching health care workers from China and The Dominican Republic, or South Korean, South Asian, and Russian MBA students, there were Heroes, Comics, and Innocents among them.

## A TYPE IS NOT A STRAIGHT JACKET

We all want to feel unique. Usually right after administering an assessment tool during a training, I sense an uncomfortable tension in the room. Even though the individual participants acknowledge that the information they are reading about themselves is spot on, they are disturbed by the concept of being pigeonholed. Just like my actor friends complaining about being typecast. People feel that being identified as a certain type locks them into certain behaviors. So I will say it now and repeat it often: No one is ONLY one type. We are usually a combination of two or three types with one type being more prominent. That dominant type can be your ticket to stardom OR it could be holding you back. Think about some of our well-known celebrities. John Wayne was always cast as a John

Wayne type. And present-day actors like Seth Rogin play a similar character in every movie he is in, but it's a great character; it's totally consistent with his physical and vocal qualities and it seems consistent with certain values he seems to embody. If we look back at the VIA strengths, we could identify his strengths as being hope, a sense of wonder, and, of course, humor. He brings those qualities to every role and it has made him a trusted, bankable actor.

Like Seth Rogin and John Wayne, some of us know our strengths and know how to make the most of them. When I meet clients whose default types serve them well and are consistent with the values that they want to project, my job is to coach them in ways to better define, refine, and communicate those strengths. I might also work with them to try on qualities from other types that might be useful in helping them become even more effective communicators in other areas of their lives.

When I find that a client's default type conflicts with his or her values and distracts from the ability to communicate effectively, we will work together to eliminate or replace the distracting habits and try on or adopt the qualities of a type that will represent that client better, helping him or her shine.

I want to stress that this is not about changing who a person is. It is about changing how the person presents him-or herself when they want to or need to achieve a desired effect. For example, Shai is still in my DNA. In fact, to this day, with as much as I know about communication, around my family and old friends of the family, Shai is front and center. And in certain new or stressful situations that may mimic my childhood, Shai might also show up. The difference now is that when I need to, I have trained myself to marshall other resources and behave in ways that will have a more effective result. The way you present yourself is completely within your power.

*"Divas do it, golfers do it, pilots do it, violists do it, sprinters do it, soldiers do it, surgeons do it, astronauts do it ... only business people think it isn't necessary to train."* —TOM PETERS

Because you bought this book, I assume you recognize and appreciate the need for training and are eager to identify your strengths and weakness and to find out what resources you need to help elevate the way you communicate. We'll start by helping you discover your ActorType.

# PART I

# EXPLORING THE NINE ACTORTYPES

*What to expect in this chapter*

## The Breakdown

When directors or producers are casting a film or TV show, one of the first things they do is write a description of the character they are looking for. This description, called a "Breakdown," is distributed to agents, managers, and casting directors. It's called a Breakdown because it breaks down the qualities an actor needs to have in order to effectively portray a specific character or type envisioned by the writer and/or director.

To describe the different ActorTypes, I've created my own Breakdown. I've listed qualities of the nine different types and have explained how each of those types can become successful, sought-after superstar speakers, presenters, and communicators. Look through the list: read the characteristics, the values, and the examples. Then ask yourself in which role you find yourself most often cast (You may be one type at work and a completely different type at home.) Which role feels most comfortable? Which role or roles do you aspire to? Are you an Innocent who secretly wishes to be a Villain? Or a Curmudgeon hiding a Super Hero inside of you? Note that there is a fair amount of overlap and most people are a combination of two or more types. But if you're being completely honest, you'll recognize your natural default type. It's usually the type that shows up in stressful situations.

When you identify your dominant ActorType, ask yourself if that dominant type needs to be rewritten or edited. Does it feel harder and harder to communicate in the way that your default ActorType communicates? Do you feel you've made significant changes in your life that are not reflected in the way you present yourself now?

Discovering your ActorTypes will help you own and celebrate the qualities that work for you, which will help make all your communication more authentic and powerful. By learning and identifying your ActorType(s), you, like countless celebrities, will be on your way to superstardom.

### Fatal Flaws and Director's Notes

In screenwriting classes, one of the first things you are taught is that once you've identified your lead character you must find out that character's Fatal Flaws, so that by the end of your film your character can have a transformation. In mythology the Fatal Flaw is often referred to as the character's Achilles' heel.

Once you've identified your type or types, look over the Fatal Flaws listed below that type's description, to see if you recognize any of those flaws in your own communication style. If so, continue to the Director's Notes and discover ways to overcome the flaws that might be holding you back.

*"As human beings, our greatness lies not so much in being able to remake the world as in being able to remake ourselves"* – Mahatma Gandhi

# HERO/HEROINE

FADE IN:

A BLACK AND WHITE IMAGE-CLOSE of a FIGHTER being HIT, jaw distending too far, an impossible angle. Time stands still.

The capacity crowd is on its feet. That WINNER with his fist in the air is wiry, not too tall, not too heavy. The kind of fighter you'd say had a lot of heart. Meet JIM BRADDOCK.

Above is the introduction of Russell Crowe's character in the script for the film *Cinderella Man*. Is there any doubt that Jim Braddock will be the Hero of this story?

You immediately know the Hero in most films by the focus of the camera, the way he or she is lit, and the framing of the shot around them. The Hero, as we all know, is the star or lead of the show or film. The story revolves around them. The events of the story happen to them. Screenwriters are encouraged first and foremost to chart out the "hero's journey."

Some of you may be thinking: as a presenter, aren't we always supposed to be the Hero? The short answer is – no. Though it is important and useful to adopt many of the Hero's attributes, you can be an extremely effective presenter and communicator without having the Hero as your dominant ActorType. Think back on some of your favorite movies. Is it always the lead actor that is the most memorable, the most endearing, the most interesting even? In the 2008 Batman movie, *The Dark Knight*, the movie is stolen by the villain, the Joker. In TV shows like *30 Rock* and *The Office and Seinfeld*, many of the supporting characters are infinitely more interesting than the leads. Many people think they need to cast themselves as Hero types, even if they are not. There can be just as much power and charm in a Villain or a Sex Symbol as there is in most Heroes. So be completely honest with yourself when looking over the Hero qualities and the qualities of our other ActorTypes.

**Famous Heroes/Heroines:** Barack Obama, Bill Clinton (sometimes – though he also has a strong Villian type lurking underneath), Bette Davis, Clark Gable, Angelina Jolie, Katharine Hepburn, Daniel Craig, Matt Damon, Russell Crowe, to name only a few.

**Corresponding Archetypes:** Anima/Animas, Knight, King, Warrior, God, Hero

**DiSC Profile:** Influencer

**Important Values:** Bravery, Persistence, Integrity, Social Intelligence, Leadership

The Hero is Charisma personified. Charisma is derived from the word "Charism," which means the divine energy that gives us power. And the word Charism comes from the Greek word for "gift." Heroes/Heroines usually have energy, power, and a gift for engaging an audience.

*QUALITIES OF A HERO*

- Commands attention the second he enters a room.
- Is given a lot of responsibility even without asking for it and sometimes without wanting it.
- Is usually able to handle the responsibility given.
- Even when things start off rocky, Heroes are able to turn lemons into lemonade.
- Is able to establish instant credibility and likeability.
- Speaks well extemporaneously and has an impressive vocabulary.
- Voice: Strong, steady.
- Body Language: solid and erect posture and makes strong direct eye contact.

*THE HERO'S FATAL FLAWS:*

- Can seem one-dimensional and boring if not in touch with vulnerability
- Can sometimes be seen as aloof or uninterested

- Can feel lost when not the center of attention and may try to "upstage" other "cast members"
- Can rely too much on charisma and stop taking the listener into account
- Can take on more responsibility than they are able to handle and wind up disappointing their audience, colleagues, or bosses.

*DIRECTOR'S NOTES FOR THE HERO:*

**Differentiate yourself:** Common feedback beginning screenwriters hear is that their Hero or lead character is too "one-dimensional." The result is that you get a screenplay in which an attractive person does interesting things but does not seem like an interesting person. This usually happens because the writer does not give us enough specific information about what makes the character tick. Many Hero types are slow to own their charisma, or tend to take it for granted. If you are a Hero ActorType you need to get very clear about the specific qualities you have that set you apart and learn how to express those qualities. Drill down to discover if you are intelligent vs. wise, sophisticated vs. debonair – there are subtle differences. Uncover, hone, and readily share your personal story and make it interesting, and emotionally charged.

**Be Vulnerable:** A movie Hero usually doesn't change until his fatal flaw has been brought to light and dealt with. When an audience is aware of a Hero's flaws, it makes the Hero instantly more likeable and the audience is more inclined to support and root for him.

Don't be afraid to reveal your Achilles' heel when appropriate – get comfortable talking about your struggles and the things you have overcome. This will draw your listeners in.

**Involve Your Audience:** Heroes are accustomed to being loved at first sight. So they sometimes forget that their listeners often need that love reciprocated. Think about your listeners: What do **they** need? What do **they** want to hear? What can you **give** them? Make your presentations and meetings as interactive as possible. Be sure to use your excellent eye contact to read the faces and body language of your listeners. If they are giving you blank stares, fidgeting, or looking at their programs, be willing to adjust your presentation by employing some audience involvement techniques. (see chapter 18)

The only reason you are presenting something or communicating with someone should be because you want to have an effect. You have something to share with them. Most Heroes know this but because they are often admired just for showing up, it's easy for them to forget and fall into bad habits, like talking **at** instead of talking **to** and presenting rather than engaging. Remember to concentrate on what you have to give and what effect you want to have, not on the response you're going to get or how effective you are.

**Work on Active Listening:** Because they are very verbal and well spoken, it's easy for Heroes to dominate a conversation or to be thinking of answers or solutions while the other person is speaking.

Work on adding deliberate pauses to your conversations so that other people will feel more comfortable chiming in. And when they do chime in, be sure to employ active listening techniques like nodding, smiling, and paraphrasing some of the words or phrases you heard so that your partner feels acknowledged and understood.

**Share the Spotlight:** Even though in movies and TV shows, Heroes have the lion's share of the screen time, they are rarely in every single scene. That is because in order to have a fully realized story, an audience or listener needs to hear other points of view. Be conscious of and appreciative of your "costars." Be sure to acknowledge the contributions of others on your team and when possible give them an opportunity to shine. Resist the temptation to micromanage your meetings and dominate your team presentations. And if you don't have a team or a costar, be sure to gather statistics and research from varied sources so your listener doesn't feel that it's your way or the highway. I was at a screening for the movie *Defiance,* which starred Daniel Craig, Liev Schreiber, and Jamie Bell. During the Q & A session with Schreiber and Bell, Bell talked about a climactic scene that had been written for Daniel Craig. After rehearsing the scene with Craig, the director thought the scene might work with the newcomer, Jamie Bell. Did Craig kick and scream and refuse to give up his star turn? He did not. He realized that the film would benefit if Bell took that moment. Now that's a Hero.

**Learn to filter and say no:** Just because you can be a font of knowledge, a reliable resource, and a welcome addition to most guest lists doesn't mean that you have to say yes to every opportunity or social event presented to you. Take a good look at your values and your goals and filter each invitation you receive through those values and goals. If sitting on a particular board or going to a particular event does not align with your values or your mission or your schedule, learn how to politely decline. Saying no will prevent you from burning out and weakening your effectiveness.

# THE INGÉNUE/INNOCENT:

One dictionary definition of an ingénue is "a naïve character in a drama." And indeed, in most cases, the on-screen ingénue is innocent, sweet, kind, and generous to a fault. Ingénues/Innocents are mostly thought of as female, but male ingénues/innocents exist. Think Mickey Rooney, or Kenneth on the NBC television series *30 Rock*. There is also not a definitive cutoff age for an innocent. I have a friend in her 60s who is still working her Ingénue ActorType. Betty White could be seen as a perennial Ingénue before she developed to perfection her Villain qualities. See also Andy Spitzer from *The 40-Year-Old-Virgin*.

CAL

So what did you get into? [this weekend]

ANDY

Well, I just kind of hung out. On Friday when I got home, I really wanted an egg salad sandwich, and I was just obsessing about it. So Saturday I went out and got like a dozen eggs and boiled them all. I spent probably three hours making the mayonnaise and the onions and paprika and all the accouterments and by the time I was done, I just didn't feel like eating it.

The entire conceit of this Judd Apatow – Steve Carell movie was based on an Innocent learning to adopt the qualities of more demonstrative ActorTypes.

Do not make the mistake of equating ingénues with pushovers, however. Ingénues are usually so committed to their beliefs they will fight passionately for them to the very end. In *The 40-Year-Old-Virgin*, Andy Spitzer was determined to find love on his own terms.

True Innocents and Ingénues are rare in Hollywood these days. Writers have a tendency to turn innocent youthful characters into closet villains. However, if you look closely, you will discover ingénues in your environment. You may even find that you have a bit of the ingénue in you.

**Famous Ingénues:** Young Judy Garland, Shirley Temple, Zooey Deschanel, Kenneth in *30 Rock*, Carol Channing, Debbie Reynolds, Doris Day, Jim Nabors, Mickey Rooney, Ron Howard, Betty White, some early Steve Martin roles, *Forrest Gump*.

**Corresponding Archetypes:** The Child, The Great Mother

**DiSC Profile:** S – Supporter

**Important Values:** Love of learning, Vitality, Open-mindedness, Humility, Hope, Persistence, Curiosity

## Qualities of an INGÉNUE

- Asks a lot of questions and can be extremely detail oriented
- Has a wide-eyed excitement about new things and assignments
- Eternal Optimist; Does not allow him/herself to become bitter or jaded when things go wrong
- Has a fresh take on old, tired ideas
- Is honest, loyal, and committed
- Tends to smile even in the toughest times
- Voice: Speaks in soft tones and /or in higher pitches
- Body Language: Straight standing and seated posture that can sometimes appear stiff; eye contact can be almost too direct at times; have tendency to be close-talkers

## Ingénue's Fatal Flaws

- Don't always speak up about their views and ideas
- Can choose to take the back seat in the presence of the Hero or Villain
- Can appear weak or spineless and therefore can be easily dismissed

- Can appear less intelligent than they are and therefore may not be taken seriously
- Their views sometimes can sound airy-fairy and out of left field
- Their constant questioning can become annoying

*DIRECTOR'S NOTES:*

**Let Your Light Shine:** As an Ingénue you are committed to seeing things in brighter colors than others. You have a unique, unjaded, and fresh viewpoint. But sometimes you find yourself overwhelmed by other types who are able to assert a more "realistic" opinion. Because Ingénues typically like to avoid confrontation, they fear using any communication style that might come off as aggressive. My favorite definition for the differences between Aggressive Submissive, and Assertive is this: Aggressive means "I'm important and you're not." Submissive means "You're important and I'm not." Assertive means "We're both important."

Remember that it is very IMPORTANT for people to hear your view. What would a movie look like shot in only one color? I often coach my Ingénue clients to think of their communication as though they are in a life-or-death situation and their opinions or viewpoint could save their life or the life of someone they love. This brings a certain urgency to their presentation style that pushes them to a more powerful delivery. What do you hold near and dear? Imagine it being taken away from you if you do not clearly state your position or opinion.

**Give the Facts:** Ingénues tend to have an endearing natural charm about them. They therefore have less need for rapport-building techniques than do some of the other types. However, their form of charm can also sometimes be mistaken for childishness, so they are often taken less seriously. You can counteract having your charm overwhelm your intelligence by remembering to use statistics and quotes within your presentation and communication. You enjoy doing research and discovering unusual information, so pepper your communication with hard undisputable facts. This will counter your listener's instinct to discredit your intellect.

**Work on Your Voice:** Most Ingénues have a higher-pitched or softer-toned voice. Unfortunately, because of our Lizard brains, people who speak softly or in their upper registers are not taken as seriously as are their stronger-voiced colleagues. Remember, the voice counts for 38% of your message's effectiveness. Your voice and the energy expressed in your voice are a reflection of the energy and power you command. As much as I believe in people being authentic and congruent with their strengths and values, I have never met anyone with an Ingénue's voice who sounded confident, competent, and powerful. If your voice is higher pitched, nasal, or if you tend to be soft-spoken, I strongly suggest you devote a considerable amount of time to strengthening your voice. You can use the Vocal exercises in Chapter 16 of this book, purchase my *Vocal Workout* CD, or hire a coach – but I guarantee that the investment of time and or money will be worth it.

**Beware of Oversharing:** Unlike the Hero, Innocents or Ingénues usually have no problem appearing vulnerable. But sometimes Innocents will give their listeners too much information, as in the above excerpt from The 40-Year-Old-Virgin. Be aware of the time your listener has and the appropriateness of the information you are sharing. Think of the bottom line for the particular communication or presentation you are delivering. Does the information you are sharing help the listener understand the bottom line or does it distract from the bottom line? Learn to read your listener's body language. If he/she is looking lost or confused, dial back the details.

**Don't be a "Close Talker":** Because innocents tend to be less guarded themselves, they sometimes fail to notice when they are encroaching into someone else's space. There is a comfortable distance for business conversations. Most people feel that an arm's length or two or three feet is an appropriate distance. In seated situations, draw an imaginary line down the center of the desk or table between you and the person across from you. Be aware of staying on your side of the line. You can lean in, but only as far as the imaginary center line. Each person is different. Notice if people are leaning away from you or moving back when they speak to you. Take that as a cue to keep your distance.

**Preface Your Questions:** Ingénues ask a lot of questions, not because they're not smart but because they want to be certain they get it right. The number of questions an Ingénue asks can seem excessive to certain types like Super Heroes and Curmudgeons. It might be useful for you in such situations to preface your barrage of questions with an acknowledgement: "I'm very detail oriented so I tend to ask a lot of questions." OR "I get exactly what you're saying and I have quite a few questions. I hope you don't mind." OR after you've already asked quite a few questions: "Thank you for being so patient. It's important for me to get all the details" or "I want to make certain I understand you…"

**Preface Your Ideas:** Since you often have original, out-of-the-ordinary ideas and points of view, to be sure that your listener is prepared to take them in. Preface your more unusual ideas with a statement that prepares your listeners: "I understand what you're saying and I'm wondering if you thought about … " " I love where this is going and I have a crazy idea … " "This might seem out of the box but …"

# THE VILLAIN

Many of you may be wondering why I'm devoting an ActorType to the Villain. Isn't the Villain the "bad guy"? What useful qualities could a villain bring to a presentation? Who would want to be identified as a Villain? However, if you think about the qualities a good villain has, you will understand why a Villain can be a compellingly effective communicator. A Villain is riveting, complex, intimidating, and powerful. These are qualities that come in handy as a leader or presenter. Think about the Villains that you love to hate. The two obvious examples are Heath Ledger in *The Dark Knight* and Meryl Streep in *The Devil Wears Prada*. But before that, there was Anthony Hopkins in *Silence of the Lambs*, and Boris Karloff and Bela Lugosi in the Frankenstein and Dracula movies.

The Hero uses his or her charm and charisma to garner attention. The Villain has a different type of charisma. The Villain makes people wonder whether he or she is going to torture them, or let them off easy. That kind of charisma, if used well, can make a presenter extremely engaging. One of the most common situations I see is a client showing up as a Hero when he or she might be more authentic and effective as a Villain.

I was once at a three-day conference which focused on how to influence people. Over the course of those three days, I saw approximately 15 different presenters. One presenter who really stood out, and whom I will always remember, was a gentleman who was clearly in touch with and effectively used his Villain qualities. He walked onto the stage and glared at us for a full minute and a half, which is an eternity in a large room. Then he made a statement dripping with arrogance – something about how great he was at what he did. He paused for a few more seconds, longer than most people would feel comfortable pausing, while the audience took in his statement and his audacity for having made it. Then, when the audience expected him to apologize or say his arrogance was an act, he proceeded to make another arrogant statement. I think this time it was about how much money he made or how much his suit cost. By then, the entire audience, all 500 or so of us, were completely and utterly in love with him. Why? Because he was unabashedly embracing his villain and we couldn't help but be attracted to it.

**Famous Villains**: The Joker, Jack Nicholson, Glenn Close, Hannibal Lecter, James Spader, Anjelica Huston, Christopher Walken, Alec Baldwin, Sigourney Weaver (later years)

**Corresponding Archetypes**: The Shadow, The Trickster

**DiSC Profile**: D – Dominance

**Important Values**: Bravery, Vitality, Leadership, Humor

*QUALITIES OF THE VILLAIN...*

- Attracts attention when walking into the room – but unlike the hero, the Villain may make the audience or listeners feel a bit uncomfortable
- Has a devilish smile which he/she doles out judiciously
- Has a quick wit and a sharp tongue
- Has an answer for everything; likes to have the last word
- Tends to act superior to everyone and everything
- Has sex appeal but doesn't flaunt it
- Compels an audience to pay attention
- Voice: Can be loud and booming, or have a purring or serpentine hissing sound
- Body Language: Assumes a physical position of power or intimidation – having audiences look up to him/her or invading listener's personal space by standing too close

*VILLAIN'S FATAL FLAWS*

- Arrogance can sometimes turn off as many people as it turns on
- Sense of humor can hurt feelings and scare off listeners
- Can be all bravado and no substance
- Won't admit when he/she is wrong or doesn't know something
- If not aware of or willing to own or adapt his/her Villain qualities, can seem hostile and intimidating

**Show Glimpses of Your Inner Teddy Bear:** Most villains have one. When I work with Villain types, I NEVER try to turn them into Heroes. I will coach them to choose times to turn down the volume, literally. If you have a booming voice, choose sections of your speech or conversation to speak more quietly. If you tend to purr or hiss, take some moments to clearly articulate and project.

I watched a Villain type deliver a presentation at an event at which I was also a speaker. His voice was rough and gravelly and he seemed to shout most of his message in a very aggressive tone. Even though it only lasted 30 minutes, my assistant said afterwards that she was offended by his presentation. She had felt yelled at. (It didn't help that his content was not very rich or informative.) This Villain type would have benefited from taking more pauses, lowering his volume in some sections, and occasionally exchanging the relentless staccato rhythm he had for a slower more melodic one.

**Do Your Research:** Like the Super Hero and the Sex Symbol, the Villain often relies on sheer presence to make an impact. Villains need to be very sharp with their content because people who may be instinctually turned off by their style will HAVE to respect them if they show an ability to communicate important, relevant, and appropriate information.

**Feign Humility:** A person with a true Villainous default setting has real difficulty admitting mistakes or acknowledging an opposing view. So when I'm working with a Villain, I coach them to "act as if" they care by applying the following techniques.

- **Build pauses** into the communication. A pause will allow the listener/audience to breath, relax, and take in what was actually said. Villains can be intimidating and can overwhelm an audience, so pauses will give your audience or listener a much needed break.
- It's also important to build in pauses before answering a question. Most people are used to answering questions immediately after they are asked. Everyone needs to learn to add a thoughtful pause before a response, but it's especially important for the Villain.
- **Acknowledge an opposing or contradictory viewpoint** before you state your own usually strong opinion.

Example:

Instead of: "We all just need to take a pay cut!"

Try: "I know you feel we need to lay off 15 more people in order to make up our budget deficit. I strongly believe that we can meet our budget by each and every one of us agreeing to a pay cut!"

Again, acknowledging another person's point of view before speaking is an important technique for all types, but it is a necessity for Villains. Even though they may still come across as arrogant, they will come across as a being a little more self-aware and empathetic.

**Acknowledge and own your Villainous qualities:** Many successful, self-aware Villains make a habit of letting their colleagues and listeners know right up front that their sense of humor may be a bit unorthodox and that they can come on a little strong. If you are a true Villain, acknowledging these qualities won't sound like an excuse, which would be totally out of character, but they will sound like a fact of life that your listener can accept or not. People will be forewarned and will usually respond more favorably to your humor, tone, and demeanor.

**Learn to respect other points of view:** This can be a tough one for most Villains. They really don't understand how other people's minds work and how other people can think so completely differently. I recently took a practitioner certification course in Neural Linguistic Programming, an approach to communication, personal development and psychotherapy. There are two presuppositions in the practice of Neural Linguistic Programming that Villains should try to keep in mind and operate from: 1) "Respect others' model of the world" and 2) "People always make the best choices available to them, given their unique model of the world and of the situation."

The next time someone gives you feedback or a suggestion, PAUSE before responding, reflect on all you know about the person who just made the suggestion or gave the feedback, imagine being that person, and then imagine the situation from that person's point of view. Then ask yourself, how much would it really cost you to try on or consider that other person's point of view. You might be surprised to find out that in those few moments of breathing and considering, you might just discover one or two useful things you could learn from that other person.

# THE COMIC

Comic sidekicks and comic leads are staples in the entertainment world. In buddy movies, one character is usually the "straight man" and the other the comic relief. And as the term comic relief implies, this character is responsible for relieving dramatic tension from situations before the situation becomes too heavy. Depending on the film, the sidekick is often more memorable than the lead. A comic lead, or comic hero, uses his or her humor to get out of awkward situations and to basically cope with things that normal people might find stressful. Similarly, an effective Comic ActorType uses his or her humor to communicate information that might seem difficult and stressful and also knows how to get in touch with his/her serious side when it's needed. Having the Comic ActorType as the dominant type is rare but many other types have a humorous side. You know a Comic ActorType when you see one because they will usually lead with their humor.

**Famous Comics:** Robin Williams, Chris Rock, Eddie Murphy, Judy Holliday, Sandra Bullock, Debra Messing, Tina Fey, Carol Burnett, Kristen Wiig, Will Smith.

**Corresponding Archetype:** The Trickster

**DiSC Profile:** i, S Influencer, Supporter

**Important Values:** Open-mindedness, Vitality, Humility, Humor

*QUALITIES OF THE COMIC:*

- Makes people smile sometimes simply by his/her presence
- Can find the humor in any situation
- Often finds self in awkward and/or embarrassing situations
- Not outwardly affected by other people's views and opinions
- Voice: Extreme pitch variety and unique vocal quality in speaking voice OR total monotone delivery
- Body Language: Has a quirky gait and or slightly awkward posture; not great at eye contact

*COMIC FATAL FLAWS:*

- Doesn't always know when enough is enough and can exhaust or exasperate audience or listeners
- Can offend people with inappropriate humor
- Can use humor to keep him-or herself from engaging in relationships
- Can miss or trivialize important details
- Can care more about being liked than doing a good job

*DIRECTING NOTES FOR THE COMIC*

**Be Vigilant about Eye Contact:** Many Comic lead/sidekicks are so busy thinking about their next joke that they look up into their own heads instead of into their listener's eyes. Not giving your listener eye contact gives the impression of not being engaged and keeps relationships more distant.

**Develop Top-Notch Listening Skills:** In conversation, be sure to employ the power of the pause. Pause and count to five before you respond. Paraphrase what you've heard the other person say to make sure you are really responding to what is being said or asked and not just giving the first pithy or humorous response that comes into your head.

**Get the Facts:** Be sure to do your research and use well-documented facts when giving a presentation. It's okay to sandwich them between appropriate humor, but people do not usually come to presentations to hear stand-up. You must include substance and rational arguments.

**Add to Your Vocal Repertoire:** Vocal variety is something I strive to bring out in all of my clients. However, for Comics, I suggest they experiment with using a more even and steady tone for certain communications. People will be able to take you more seriously when you can move from your quick-paced, musical delivery (or slow-paced monotone one) to a stronger, steadier, more powerful tone.

**Don't Force it:** Most true Comics can make people smile just by walking onto the stage. It's an innate natural gift. Trust it. You don't have to force the humor or have your audience rolling in the aisle to know that you are doing a good job. So breathe and "be"; don't "do." You'll be a much more effective and likeable presenter.

**Get Comfortable with Not Getting Feedback:** This is directly related to the above note. If you are not getting the response you feel you would like, it doesn't mean that you are "bombing." It may mean that the listener is taking in the information but either doesn't find it as amusing as you do, or feels that you are too invested in his/her response and are therefore withholding it. Be more invested in the information that you are giving and less invested in the response you are getting.

# WHIZ KID/KNOW-IT-ALL

Whiz Kids, Geeks, Nerds, and Know-it-Alls have always been part of the movies and TV. At the writing of this book, one of the hottest sitcoms on Television is *The Big Bang Theory* – its entire starring cast is made up of Whiz Kids, Nerds, and Geeks. Think Mr. Spock and Data of *Star Trek*. Even Cary Grant played some great nerds in his day. With the advances in technology we have a whole new interesting crop of Whiz Kids like the computer geeks on *24, NCIS,* and almost every other television procedural and detective or mystery movie. A Whiz Kid's function is to provide all the technical answers and know-how that the Hero is too busy to think of or research. It is often the Whiz Kid who saves the day, while the Hero gets most of the credit. As in this scene from *Star Trek V: The Final Frontier.*


ANGLE - KIRK, SPOCK, AND McCOY


Sinking lower, on the verge of capture.


KIRK
Spock ... the booster rockets.


SPOCK
If I activate them, we will be propelled
upward at unpredictable speed.

KIRK
(an order)
Fire the boosters!

Spock hits the boosters. With an explosion of power and noise they shoot skyward like a bullet.

Our heroes are an upward blur that shows no sign of stopping. Spock hits "the brakes" and they stop barely one floor from the ceiling, bobbing in mid-air. Kirk and McCoy are white as sheets.

SPOCK
I am afraid I overshot our mark by one level.

McCOY
Nobody's perfect.

Often Whiz Kids do not acknowledge or take credit for all the important work they contribute to their bosses, colleagues, and families. And because they are so unassuming, they often get overlooked for promotions and awards.

**Famous Whiz Kids:** Bill Gates, Mr. Spock, John Nash *(A Beautiful Mind)*, Cynthia Nixon, Tony Shalhoub *(Monk)*, Peter Parker *(Spider-Man)*, Don Cheadle in the *Ocean's* movies.

**Corresponding Archetype:** The Wise Old Man/Woman

**DiSC Profile:** C-Calculator

**Important Values:** Curiosity, Love of learning, Perspective, Integrity, Prudence

QUALITIES OF THE WHIZ KID

- Has a failsafe memory for facts
- Loves doing research
- Is dependable and responsible
- Is organized and exacting
- Voice: Tends to speak fast and /or in a monotone or with a specific repetitive rhythm
- Body Language: Posture is sometimes hunched or round-shouldered, tends to avoid direct eye contact.

WHIZ KID FATAL FLAWS:

- Has little or no sense of humor
- Misses nuances in communication
- Can be dismissed as being boring
- Can be disliked for being a know-it-all or a killjoy

- Trouble seeing or acknowledging points of view other than his/her own
- Has the habit of "data dumping"

*DIRECTOR'S-NOTES FOR WHIZ KIDS:*

**Find Emotional Connections**: Yes, you have an incredible amount of valuable information to share, but you have to make a connection with your audience or else they won't be able to take any of that information in. It's super important for Whiz Kids to learn to develop rapport and to employ audience involvement techniques. For the past eight years, I've been working with a company that helps train financial advisors. Sometimes as a single woman and sometimes with a man playing my husband, I role-play meetings with new financial advisors. In this work I often encounter Whiz Kids. They know the investment business inside and out. However, sitting across the desk from them can be a real snooze fest. I often feel talked at instead of talked to. And no matter how convincing the information is, I am rarely interested in having a second meeting with them. Most of the time, I get confused midway through and actually lose the ability to discern what they are talking about.

**Watch Your Jargon**: Remember to make the information you are sharing accessible to all and jargon free. You may know exactly what you mean when you use an acronym or the technical term for something, but if there's a 1% chance that your listener may not understand, break what you are saying down into everyday

English. There's an old adage used in many acting classes and screenwriting classes "Less is More" Leave your listeners asking for more, not overwhelmed with too much.

**Stand with Power:** If your posture is slouched, you will give the impression of being unsure of yourself, and your material and all of the important information you deliver will be more carefully scrutinized and judged. That's if it's heard at all. Remember that the verbal part of the message, the part you care so dearly about, can account for as little as 7% of the communication.

**Make Strong Eye Contact:** If you do not make eye contact with the people you are speaking with, they may assume you are insincere and possibly not trustworthy. When a speaker appears insecure or shifty by not making eye contact, the information delivered becomes suspect.

**Acknowledge Gray Areas:** Facts are king to the Geek, but it's important for you to acknowledge that there are "more things in heaven and earth than are dreamt of in your philosophy," to quote Shakespeare. State facts but don't force them down the a listener's throat. Allow for the possibility that your listener may not believe you, or may have a different viewpoint. Give as much evidence as possible to support your statements. But when what you are saying is actually an informed opinion, tell your listener it's your opinion and don't state it as a fact.

**Smile!** It's amazing how a simple thing like a smile can lighten up a Whiz Kid's presentation.

**Practice Spontaneity**: I like to recommend that my Geek clients take an acting or improvisation class so they can get in touch with another side of their personality.

**Do Vocal Exercises**: Audiences quickly turn off and stop listening to a presentation delivered in a monotonous voice. Because the Whiz Kid usually has so much valuable information, it's important to work on the communications skills that will increase the chances of that communication being received. Think of your speeches as pieces of music. Stress words and phrases by going up or down in pitch, speaking faster or slower, or lengthening or shortening the pronunciation (See exercises on page 149 or my *Vocal Workout* CD)

One of my most successful coaching experiences was turning a Whiz Kid/Buddy ActorType into a Super Hero. This client had a long and successful career as an accountant (the career definition of a Geek). She had recently started an independent business in which she would consult and give expert testimonies about accounting practices for corporate disputes. While she was working with a group of lawyers who had hired her to give testimony on an important trial they were involved with, the lawyers started to voice concern over her delivery, fearing that it did not seem confident enough. That's when she called on me. This client knew her facts cold but she was not coming off as confident or authoritative enough, especially since she would have to deliver a deposition with lawyers from the opposing side grilling her for 10 HOURS! The most obvious issue was what the lawyers were calling vocal tick. It was a very subtle intake of air that sounded almost like a stifled laugh. She had the habit of making that sound after statements that were particularly strong or powerful. She also had an ingrained habit of upspeaking – making everything sound like a question – and her voice was placed in her throat, not her diaphragm. Through vocal exercises and mental visualizations, we were able to find a vocal tone that sounded strong, assertive, and powerful. We also needed to address the Buddy side of her personality, which made her tend to give out more information than was called for. We made sure that she gave just the facts and nothing but the facts. I was thrilled when she emailed me after her 10 hours on the stand to say that it was a tremendous success. The lawyers who hired her were extremely impressed.

# SUPER HERO/ACTION HERO

If you are wondering how the Super Hero differs from our Hero, think of the difference between John Wayne and Bruce Willis or between Bette Davis and Sigourney Weaver. A Hero can saunter into a room and get noticed, but the Super Heroes burst into a room and force you to notice them. Or they enter surreptitiously and then attack when they are faced with a battle that needs to be won. The Super Hero feels compelled to take action to right wrongs, to fight injustice, to defend honor. Even though most Heroes may feel compelled to talk about and rally support around righting these wrongs, the Super Hero is willing to risk physical harm to do it. This quality adds a different energy and focus that sets the Super Hero ActorType apart from the Hero ActorType.

**Famous Super Heroes:**

Jason Bourne, Superman, Batman, Wonder Woman, Sigourney Weaver *(Alien)* Uma Thurman *(Kill Bill)* Clint Eastwood, Nancy Grace (TV shock journalist) Don Quixote

Note: Catwoman and Spiderman are not true Super Heros, because their "powers" and thus their actions are the result of something happening TO them. It wasn't a choice.

**Corresponding Archetype:** The Hero, The Persona

**DiSC Profile:** D – Dominance

**Important Values:** Persistence, Integrity, Leadership

*QUALITIES OF THE SUPER HERO:*

- Intense, committed, and passionate
- Has a strong, unwavering moral and/or ethical code
- Is willing to go above and beyond to accomplish a goal
- Will research and investigate every angle and detail of a project
- Will pursue any goal or lead that looks the least bit promising
- Voice: Strong, powerful, and unwavering
- Body Language: Are agile and quick on their feet and like to move during presentations. Have intense and prolonged eye contact

*SUPER HERO FATAL FLAWS:*

- Will not take no for an answer and therefore can be stubborn and downright pigheaded.
- Has a tendency to see danger or trouble where there isn't any
- Can come on too strong and frighten supporters away
- Can worry an issue like a dog gnawing a bone

- Can feel alienated because so few people share their intensity

**Listen**: Really listen to what others are saying. Like the comic, try paraphrasing back what you hear. Then take a breath before you jump in and try to fix the other person. It could be that they just want to be heard and not "rescued." During a presentation, listening translates into pauses. Add pauses often. Many of your ideas are so strong and sometimes so radical that your listeners will need extra time to be able to process them.

**See the Forest**: Super Heroes tend to spend most of their time felling individual trees and fail to step back to take a look at the whole forest. It's important when creating a presentation or chairing a meeting that you acknowledge the other points of view and possible objections. In order to do that, you have to be able to see the other side. Think of the people and issues in your life as individual puzzle pieces. If every piece of the puzzle looked exactly alike, you could never assemble it. Learn to notice and appreciate the uniqueness of each individual puzzle piece. It may not look like yours, but it has a very specific function. Find out what that function is and maybe you'll find a way to connect.

**Don't Overreact:** Yes, some issues that bug you really need to be addressed, but be sure to do thorough research and make sure of all the facts before you bring in a sledge hammer to deal with something that an ice pick could handle.

**Set Worry Limits:** Decide how much time you are going to devote to a certain task or problem; it can be hourly, daily, or weekly. But allow yourself that much time and no more to work on or worry about a project or issue.

**Explore Using a Softer Tone:** The Super Hero's strong, powerful voice and intense energy can be a real asset during certain types of presentations and conversations. However, it can also leave listeners feeling preached at and condescended to. Therefore, it's important to add lighter, more musical tones to your vocal arsenal. A lighter tone will enable listeners to feel safer and more comfortable around you and will make them more willing to see your point of view.

# THE SEX SYMBOL/SUPER MODEL

Heroes, Villains, and Super Heroes in film and TV usually have quite a bit of sex appeal. The other ActorTypes is the fact that the Sex Symbols, however, make sure that their physical attractiveness is the first thing that people notice. This is not to say that the Sex Symbol ActorType is shallow or uncaring. They may care about and be committed to some of the same issues as the Hero or Super Hero, but they are hyperaware of the importance of looking good and want to make sure they look terrific while they are expressing that commitment. They also need to know that they are being appreciated for looking good and that there is an emotional connection between them and their audience or listener. Many people have Sex Symbol as their default type based solely on biology – they are physically stunning and can effectively use their looks to become engaging communicators. However, not all physically stunning individuals are Sex Symbol ActorTypes and not all Sex Symbol ActorTypes are physically stunning.

**Famous Sex Symbols:** Marilyn Monroe, Clark Gable, Sofia Vergara, John Travolta *(Saturday Night Fever)* Raquel Welch, George Clooney, Channing Tatum

**Corresponding Archetype:** The Damsel in Distress, The Persona, The Anima/Animus

**DiSC Profile:** i S – Influencer, Supporter

**Important Values:** Creativity, Vitality, Love, Wonder

QUALITIES OF *THE SEX SYMBOL*

- Makes sure every detail is taken care of and is aesthetically pleasing
- Has very high standards. will not settle for anything that is second-rate
- Seductive – great at grabbing attention and dazzling the audience.
- Able to blind their listeners to any flaws that might exist
- Will go to great lengths and employ unique methods to get what they want
- Voice: Lilting and or seductive vocal tones. Men may have deep, sexy Barry White sound; Women can sometimes have high-pitched, childlike tone or a wispy, sultry tone.
- Body Language: Knows how to strike a pose that highlights their attractiveness. Soft focus but steady eye contact.

SEX SYMBOL FATAL FLAWS:

- Can be easily dismissed as being shallow
- Uses attractiveness as a shield, keeping intimate relationships at bay
- Can rely on attractiveness over hard work to reach a goal

- Can be judgmental of those who do not place as much emphasis on appearance
- Can be dangerously narcissistic – "It's all about me"
- Would much rather be pursued than pursue

DIRECTOR'S NOTES FOR SEX SYMBOL:

**Develop your Fourth "V":** Look over the list of VIA values and identify one or two that really speak to you. Concentrate on infusing that value into your communication style. How can you live, breathe, dress, tell stories around that value? In business and professional situations, make a point of communicating that value whenever possible. This will enable your coworkers, colleagues, and friends to realize that you are more than just a pretty face. Yes, the Visual element of communication is worth 55%; however, overfocusing on the visual has its drawbacks.

**Research and Prepare Your Content:** Many non – Sex Symbol types are conditioned to believe that if it looks good, it can't be good for you. Therefore, make sure your content is detailed and supported. We know that looking good is more than half the battle, but make sure your presentations are filled with details and substance. You don't want your colleagues or customers to feel like they've bought into "The Emperor's New Clothes"– being attracted to what you are saying because it looks and sounds good, but on closer inspection, finding that there's no substance.

**Less Is More:** Just like Whiz Kids need to trust that their content will be understood without overcommunicating it, Super Models need to trust that their attractiveness will be noticed without flaunting it. At some purely social events being overtly sexy or flirtatious can be a real asset (depending on your endgame) but in a business setting, it has its drawbacks. Sex Symbol/Super Model Actortypes don't need to completely hide their sexiness, but it's a good idea in business situations to take it down a notch, especially when it comes to wardrobe and posture. Not only will you be taken more seriously, you will also lessen the envious wrath of those less physically endowed.

**Develop an Authoritative Tone:** Since the voice is 38% of the message, develop a voice that can command attention and respect. Women who rely on their sexy, sultry tones will risk seeming flirtatious or flighty and not being taken as seriously as they might like. Men risk coming off as slick or disingenuous. Save the sultry and seductive tones for the bedroom.

**Stand on Your Own Two Feet:** When you want to get your point across, adapt the "Ready Position": Feet hip distance apart, weight slightly forward, knees slightly bent. (See Chapter 13) Standing in the Ready Position gives the appearance of strength and power. Most female Sex Symbols like to stand with one hip jutting out to the side; this may show your body off nicely but gives a much weaker impact and gives the First Brain the impression that you are a pushover. Male Sex Symbols tend to stand in the super-wide-legged Cowboy stance, which, although it looks powerful, can sometimes be off-putting.

**Embrace Diversity**: Like the Super Hero and the Comic, know that there is value in all the other Star types. The Nerd or Curmudgeon may not feel comfortable in Gucci, but may have some very worthwhile ideas to share. Learn to overlook their lack of fashion sense and give them a chance. And maybe help them out by showing them the statistics in this book and offering take them on a shopping trip. (Good luck with that!)

**Learn the Art of Pursuit:** Sex Symbols are used to getting attention for doing very little. Therefore, they can be reluctant to follow up on a lead or to reach out and ask someone for their help or their business. Learn to borrow some of the qualities of the Super Hero. Know that if you embrace your values authentically, you will not come off as being needy, incompetent, or too salesy. On the contrary, by using your abundant charm and your state-of-the-art marketing tools, you will more likely become irresistible.

# THE BUDDY

What would Thelma be without Louise? Or Starsky without Hutch? Every Hero in film or TV needs or wants a best friend. Someone who will stick by them through thick and thin; someone they can trust and rely on to point out their flaws and appreciate their good points; someone to love them unconditionally.

The Buddy ActorTypes are very effective communicators because they treat their audience or listeners like a best friend. They understand that really effective communication is not so much about being liked, as it is about helping the listeners absorb information, navigate change, and feel understood. The Buddy ActorType differs from the Hero in that unlike most Heroes, Buddies don't worry about appearing vulnerable or looking foolish. They will do anything to protect their customer or their colleague, or to get their point across.

**Famous Buddies:** Seth Rogen, Sally Field, Karl Malden, Geena Davis, Sandra Bullock, Tom Hanks

**Corresponding Archetypes:** The Mentor, The Self

**DiSC Profile:** S – Supporters

**Important Values:** Open-mindedness, Perspective, Vitality, Love, Kindness, Fairness, Forgiveness, Gratitude

*QUALITIES OF THE BUDDY*

- Great listeners
- Very dependable. Always there when you need them
- Have the ability to make the majority of people feel comfortable immediately
- As enthusiastic about other people's goals and achievements as they are about their own
- Loves to tell stories and use analogies and examples
- Is committed to excellent customer service
- Voice: Usually warm with a musical tone and rhythm
- Body Language: Has a good, open posture. Usually, Buddies naturally lean in toward the person they're speaking with; no problem with eye contact

*FATAL FLAWS*

- Can sometimes care so much for other people that they neglect taking care of their own needs
- Caring qualities can be misinterpreted and cause them to be treated as pushovers or doormats
- Can become pushy in their enthusiasm about what they believe other people should be doing
- Can be overly sensitive if they feel their support is not appreciated

- Their stories and examples can go on too long and become boring and confusing

DIRECTOR'S NOTES:

**Be Assertive NOT Submissive:** Like the Ingénue, a Buddy ActorType needs to commit the definitions of Aggressive, Submissive, and Assertive to memory. Aggressive means *I'm important and you're not.* Submissive means *You're important and I'm not.* Assertive means *We're both important.* It's commendable that you have the capacity to care so deeply about other people. However, it's just as important to care that much about yourself. Putting other people's needs and preferences above yours is not useful to you and ultimately may lead the other person to lose respect for you. We've all seen those movies where the Best Friend gets left behind or looked over. The 2011 movie *Bridesmaids* has a great example of that happening between Kristen Wiig's and Maya Rudolph's characters.

**Get to the Point:** I'm a real believer in the power of story and of using analogies and metaphors to get a point across. In fact, in Neural Linguistic Programming we often use multiple long-winded stories as a technique to effect change in a client. However, in business, in presentations, and in everyday life, it's important to learn the art of timing and how to read and react to people's body language as they listen to your stories. You may have a great point that you're getting to, but once you see your listeners fidgeting, looking away, checking their watches, you might want to think about skipping a few of the less-important details and getting to the heart of the matter. It doesn't usually matter where you were standing, or what time of day it was, or what EXACTLY happened beforehand. When time and attention spans are limited – spare us some of these painstaking details.

**Add a Touch of the Hero to Your Vocal Repertoire:** Buddy Types usually have a varied musical or soothing vocal tone to their voice. However, it's important for you to have a more assertive tone tucked away in your back pocket for when you need it. Because the Buddy ActorType likes to keep everything smooth and calm for as long as possible, they tend to bury their emotions too long. When they finally get angry, they blow, and their voice goes immediately from melodious and calm to shrill or bombastic. When you feel you need to make your feelings heard, take a deep breath, use your diaphragm, and adopt a strong, powerful, assertive – not aggressive – tone. People will be able to hear what it is that you feel strongly about and not write you off for overreacting or being hysterical.

**Learn to Separate:** One of the reasons Buddy Types get so emotional about other people's goals is that they have trouble separating from those whom they love and admire. They want so much to support those they believe in, that they neglect to see where they end and their company or other person begins. Know that you can be both supportive and separate. When someone you care about is unhappy or having a hard time, it's fine to lend a shoulder for them to lean on, but you don't need to let them bury you in their problems. Get clear on what it is you can offer them and know that you cannot solve their problem singlehandedly. Spending extra energy, time, and emotions on their problem can be draining and take important time, energy, and emotion from your own goals and needs.

**Own Your Opinion:** Buddy Types are sometimes reluctant to strongly state opinions during presentations and at meetings. They often have the tendency to talk around their points, hoping that someone will infer what it is that they are trying to say. Unfortunately, most people can't read minds, and many people who are able to decipher what you are trying to say may see this type of communication as passive aggressive and deliberately ignore it. So whereas the Villain Type and the Curmudgeon need to learn to add a little tentative language to some of their communication, the Buddy Type needs to borrow some natural direct language from other types. Instead of: "Don't you think it would be better if the reports were sent two days in advance?" Or "Where I used to work, the reports were always submitted in advance" Try: "I believe, getting the reports two days in advance will tremendously help our work flow. How can we make that happen?"

One of my clients who is a Buddy ActorType had just started in a new job as a VP at a large corporation. She had to supervise a team of three and had weekly one-on-one meetings with each of her supervisees. During one of our sessions, I found out that one of the people she supervised was often late for meetings. I was shocked to find out that when this person was late, my client would go looking for her at her desk instead of calling and making the supervisee come to her. I coached her on what to do when this situation presented itself again. She had to call the person, tell her that she was late for their meeting, and strongly state that she needed to set aside outside issues by immediately attending. Before the meeting started, my client was to say something like: "This was the fifth (or whatever specific number it was) time that you have been late for our meeting. This really does not work for me. I've set aside this time for us to review and assess your projects and when you are late that takes time away from other things I need to be doing. I need for you to respect the time I've set aside for these meetings and show up on time. Is there something preventing you from doing that?"

# SALTY VETERAN/CURMUDGEON

The lovable, sometimes cantankerous Curmudgeon is our last ActorType. And, yes the Curmudgeon can be a star. Peter Falk's Columbo was a crack detective but a Curmudgeon at heart. Walter Matthau has been a Curmudgeon practically his whole career yet still managed to star in many films. And Archie Bunker and Lou Grant made television history by being Curmudgeons. The Curmudgeon is a Hero who has dispensed with all of the trappings of being a Hero. He doesn't care about his appearance or whether or not people like him. In fact, some Curmudgeons share characteristics with the Villain, in that they don't really want to be liked. They just want to do their job and be left alone. Take the character of Harriet Korn in the television show *Harry's Law*.

INT. HARRIET'S OFFICE - DAY -

HARRIET KORN, sixtyish, sits in her well-appointed office, riveted by the CARTOON SHE WATCHES ON TELEVISION. She's also smoking a joint.

ROBERT FINEMAN, sixties, enters. He walks to the TELEVISION, TURNS IT OFF.

HARRY

I was watching that, Robert.


FINEMAN

In less than a month, you've gone from being one of the best patent lawyers in all of Cincinnati to a pot-head who sits in her office watching ... What the hell has happened?


HARRY

Well ... what's happened is, after thirty-two years of rather dedicated practice, I've come to the unfortunate if not altogether surprising conclusion that patent law is as boring as a big bowl of steaming dog – [ ]It's dull, Robert. I lead a dull life with dull partners, I consider you foremost among them, I would sooner look into a mirror and watch my teeth rot than do one more case involving patent law. As always, I value your feedback.


Other Curmudgeons share characteristics with the Super Hero, which turn them into busy bodies. They care about their job and care even more that other people are doing their jobs correctly. Think Betty White, the character of Miss Marple, or common sitcom busybodies.

**Famous Curmudgeons:** Columbo, Walter Matthau, Peter Falk, Jack Nicholson (in his later films), Betty White, Archie Bunker, Hermione Gingold, Kathy Bates (in *Revolutionary Road* and others) *Janeane Garofalo*, Tommy Lee Jones

**Corresponding Archetype:** The Persona, The Shadow

**DiSC Profile:** C-Calculator, D-Dominance

**Important Values:** Perspective, Prudence, Modesty

*QUALITIES OF THE CURMUDGEON*

- Little attention paid to appearance
- Persistent, sometimes dogged in pursuit of what they want
- Strong opinions and specific ways of doing things
- Is very observant – notices any little thing that is out of order
- Sometimes needs or pretends to need more time than others to process information
- Either asks questions until getting a satisfactory answer or doesn't ask any questions and works from assumptions
- Voice: Can speak in short, sharp, whiney tones OR in slow, deliberate monotone
- Body Language: Posture can be hunched or slouched but some Curmudgeons have the unique ability to have

good posture that is still ineffective; can be spotty with eye contact

## CURMUDGEON'S FATAL FLAWS

- Jumps too quickly to negative conclusions
- Can be intractable - so set in their ways they refuse to try new ideas
- Can be tactless in stating their opinions
- Persistence and questioning can be exhausting and annoying to non-curmudgeon types
- Lack of attention to appearance can detract from presentation and communication

## DIRECTOR'S NOTES:

**Dress for Success:** I realize that most Curmudgeons choose what they wear based on comfort. Believe it or not, there are comfortable clothes that are also stylish. Ironing and stain removal don't impact your comfort level, so indulge. True Curmudgeons will be the first to argue that they don't care if people judge them on their appearance; to heck with them they think. That's all well and good if you're a millionaire who never has to work another day in your life. However, I'm assuming that since you're reading this book that is not the case. Therefore, if you would like to improve your odds of getting more business, being taken more seriously, closing more sales, getting a well-deserved promotion, or even dating more, re-read the first chapter of this book about the Visual element of communication. Then make a sign that reads, **"Effective Communication Is 55% Visual"** and tape it to your mirror.

**Distinguish between Opinion and Fact**: A dictionary definition of opinion – "personal beliefs or judgments not founded on proof or fact." Remember this definition both in personal communication and in more formal presentations. Don't argue your opinion as fact in conversations or during presentations, acknowledge when the statements you are making are your own personal opinions. It can be as simple as adding the phrase, "I believe …" Or "In my opinion …" Of course, the other important part is admitting to yourself that it is just your opinion and that that opinion may not be shared by your listener.

**Practice the Pause and Paraphrase Technique and Polite Phraseology:** Pause and breathe before you respond. Then paraphrase the other person's words (out loud or in your head), then respond using as much Polite Phraseology as possible: "I understand you want to …" not "Are you crazy?" " I believe you meant to …" not "You're planning to do what??" "Wouldn't it be more productive if we …" not "Why on earth would we do it that way?" Would you mind considering …" not "You'd better …"

**Preface Your Questions:** It is difficult for some Curmudgeons to "get" or understand certain concepts without asking a lot of questions. That's usually because they are so convinced that their way is the right way. Sometimes, like the Ingénue/Innocent, the number of questions a curmudgeon asks can be annoying.

Therefore it's important for the curmudgeon to become aware of and sensitive to his communication partner. Preface a barrage of questions with acknowledgements like, "I'm going to need a bit more information. Do you mind if I ask you some questions?" and, again, use polite phraseology to frame the questions, instead of barking them.

SAY: "Just so that I'm clear, what's the purpose of widget # 4? NOT: What's that for?" SAY: I'm sorry but I have a few more questions. NOT: There's a lot more you need to explain.

**Ask Before You Assume:** Some Curmudgeons are the opposite of the question askers. They think asking questions is a sign of weakness. So they stay silent and assume that because they don't know something, somebody is trying to keep it from them. Curmudgeons who do this are prone to feelings of paranoia: "Everybody is out to get me or undermine me." Instead of jumping to the negative, make a conscious effort to breathe, and when you feel a negative assumption forming in your head, before that assumption takes deep root and turns into paranoia or a judgment, ask a question, remembering to use Polite Phraseology.

**Embrace Change:** This is a fast-paced world. Technological advances are here to stay. Know that everybody doesn't share your loyalty to the way things were. Frankly, people get tired of hearing things like, "But we used to do it this way ..." And "Why do we need this new system ..." It's okay to be open to new ways of doing things; if something works for you, providing it doesn't impact your job or job performance, you have the prerogative to continue doing it the "old way", but try not to judge people who choose to do it differently. There is more than one way to skin a cat. And once you learn to adopt a more engaging communication style, you might be able to share with your colleagues some of the advantages you see in doing things your way.

I recently worked with a self-proclaimed Curmudgeon. He had the hardest time accepting that people actually learn and understand things better when you can communicate to them on an emotional level. The thought of doing things like creating rapport and using analogies to talk about his services were completely foreign to him. However, I convinced him what a difference it makes to the listener and not only did he become adept at better communication, he was tapped by his company to represent it in the media. From Curmudgeon to TV personality!

# ACTORTYPES RECAP

So what is your dominant Star Type(s)? Are you 100% Curmudgeon? A Villainous Ingénue? A Sexy Super Hero? A Heroic Whiz Kid? You may be a Hero at home and a Villain at work, or an Ingénue with strangers and a Curmudgeon with those who know you well. The point to remember is that there is no right or wrong type. No type is better than another. There is only the type that you happen to embody based on both genetic and environmental influences. Whatever your type is, acknowledge it, embrace it, and own it.

**Owning and communicating in a way that is consistent with your ActorType is the surest way for you to become an authentic and successful communicator.**

While identifying and embracing your type is important, working on aspects of your style that need improvement is just as essential. I have found that the types that most often need "recasting" are (1) women who have outgrown their Ingénue persona but have not given themselves permission to step into the role of Hero; or (2) the person, male or female, who feels it important to come off as a Hero or a Buddy, when in reality they have more Villain or Curmudgeon in them and need to embrace some characteristics from those types. As you work on the following exercises in this book, you may discover an ActorType whose qualities you would like to adopt. Go for it. Try it on and see how it fits.

**WARNING**: You need to be clear and honest about your type and only adopt skills and techniques that you are comfortable with or that you have been well coached in. Adding a quality or language from another type that doesn't fit can backfire. I recently had to give feedback to a financial advisor in a training session. He had obviously been told that he should create urgency in his presentation by eliciting fear in his prospects. While I role-played a prospect, he asked me how I would feel if I suddenly didn't have my husband's income? What would I do? How would I manage? This is a technique that is appropriate for a Villain Type or possibly a Super Hero but this guy had all the underpinnings of a Buddy – he had a Teddy bear appearance and a soft, rather insecure voice and vocal tone. Those fear-based questions really turned me off. I could tell that he had adopted them from someone who told him that those tactics would work to scare a prospect into buying insurance. But as I keep saying, your words won't affect your prospects if they are not consistent with your visual and your vocal communication. This financial advisor would have been much more effective if he had said something like, "You and your husband have built a wonderful lifestyle. I would love for you to be able to continue in this lifestyle if anything were to happen to negatively affect your husband's income. That's why I believe …" That is the kind of language I would expect to hear from a Buddy Communication Type. Of course, his second mistake was not doing a better job of reading his prospects. I use a Super Hero/

Hero communication style in those kinds of role-play meetings: strong eye contact, strong handshake, strong voice, no-nonsense body language – not the type of person who would easily fall for fear tactics.

In the next section we'll take a more in-depth look at the 4 -Vs of effective communication and you will learn tips and techniques to improve and eliminate any fatal flaws that impact your communication – no matter what ActorType you are or aspire to be.

# PART II

# EXPLORING THE FOUR V'S

Knowing your ActorType is the first step in helping you communicate more authentically. However, knowing you are a Hero/Whiz Kid and having the skill set to deliver a powerful presentation can be two different things. The following section will focus on the skills and techniques that make presentations and communication shine. We will examine in detail how to polish your Visual, Vocal, and Verbal skills and how to project your Values.

# VISUAL - LOOKING THE PART

Movies use what are called "Establishing Shots" to set the mood, atmosphere, and tone of an entire film or a particular scene. It's usually a long shot of visual imagery that prepares you, gets you in the mood for what is about to come. Here is the Establishing Shot from the 2007 movie *Juno*.

EXT. CENTENNIAL LANE – DUSK

JUNO MacGUFF stands on a placid street in a nondescript subdivision, facing the curb. It's FALL. Juno is sixteen years old, an artfully bedraggled burnout kid. She winces and shields her eyes from the glare of the sun. The object of her rapt attention is a battered living room set, abandoned curbside by its former owners. There is a fetid-looking leather recliner, a chrome-edged coffee table, and a tasteless latchHooked rug featuring a roaring tiger.

Reading this and seeing how the director created this shot on the screen tells you an awful lot about the character of Juno and the tone of the movie. This is clearly a different movie and Juno is clearly a different character than say, Elle Woods in *Legally Blonde*.

Your entrance, posture, movement, and gestures along with your wardrobe create your "Establishing Shot." So let's dive into how to create a compelling Establishing Shot that will prepare your audience and get them in the mood to listen to all you have to offer.

## MAKING AN ENTRANCE

Think about your favorite award show. The camera does not wait until the star hits the stage. It captures the star from the moment she hears her name called. It watches him get out of his seat and it follows him every step until he hits the stage. Many of your audience members will do the same.

Therefore, it is important to think of the presentation, meeting, conversation, or interview starting "backstage" – meaning, well, before you enter the room.

As an actress, I've been backstage for many shows. It's always surprising to see different actors' preparation routine. Some actors keep to themselves, meditate, go over lines, and visualize. Others do loud vocal warm-ups and/or physical exercises. Still others feel fine joking and chatting with cast mates right up to the time they step out onstage. It's important to know what works best for you – what's going to help you keep energized, yet relaxed and able to deliver an engaging, effective communication.

Whatever your "backstage" routine is, remember that your audience's impression of you starts the minute you come into view, so be sure that your entrance is consistent with what it is you want to project and what it is you would like your listener to know about you.

COMMON ENTRANCES BY TYPE:

**Comics, Whiz Kid or Super Hero** – You might run or bound onto the stage, arms extended out wide or over your head. (In the case of Whiz Kids, they run or bound because the sooner they get up there, the sooner they can deliver their facts and get back off).

**Sex Symbols, Villians, Curmudgeons** – You will probably saunter slowly, deliberately, and confidently – allowing the audience to look long and hard at every aspect of you (or in the Curmudgeon's case, not caring that the audience is looking long and hard at every aspect.)

**Heroes, Ingénues, and Buddies** - Have a way of approaching energetically and purposefully, not too fast, not too slow. And making sure all eyes are watching.

Most of the above entrances can be effective as long as you are being consistent with your type. A friend of mine told me a very funny and apropos story about his campaign to get elected high school president. He had watched an opponent (who was obviously a Whiz Kid) nervously take the stage before his speech, fumble with his papers, and come across as humble, nervous, adorable, yet knowledgeable. After his first appearance, this Whiz Kid had gotten a lot of attention and support. So my friend (a clear Buddy/Super Hero type) thought he could pull the same act. You can imagine what happened. He tried to act like a Whiz Kid and reluctantly take the stage and fumble with his papers. He was met with stone-cold stares. No surprise he did not win the election.

Whatever type you are, here are some basic rules of thumb to help ensure your entrance turns heads (in the right way).

*TIPS FOR ALL TYPES TO KEEP IN MIND WHEN ENTERING A ROOM*

**Heads up** – Looking at the floor during your path to the stage or front of the room could indicate that you're not sure of yourself or that you are afraid to face what is ahead of you (the audience).

**"Pick up your feet."** – I know you may be hearing echoes of your mother's voice, but on this one, she was right. Walk with firm, even steps – shuffling or "dragging your feet" gives the impression of being reluctant, shy, unqualified, and lazy. I always recommend hard-soled shoes for important presentations. No matter how stylish they may look, standing on a cushy, soft, or rubber sole, is going to feel a lot different than standing a hard, firm, steady one. For women: I recommend a fatter, wider, chunkier heel as opposed to a spiky stiletto-type heel. You'll be able to stand firmer and feel more balanced.

**Try it out:** Put on a pair of running shoes and read the Gettysburg Address. Then read it standing on a hard leather sole and heel. Do you notice a difference?

**Interview Entrances** – When I coach my clients and students on interview skills, I will always make them go outside and practice the entrance. Entering the room during an interview is when the above two tips are extremely important. Walk in the door with purpose and energy and be ready to make eye contact and connect for a handshake. BUT – here's an important tip: after you've made the initial eye contact, be sure to break eye contact long enough for your interviewer(s) to give you the once-over. People, upon first meeting someone, will want to look them over from head to toe. We can't help it. Our lizard brains want to make sure that we take in every visual clue so that we have all the information we need to create that first impression. If you are continually maintaining eye contact as you enter the room, you don't allow the other person to do his due diligence of giving you the once-over. So … enter, smile, and maybe as you approach the desk, discover something very important about your sleeve or your briefcase/purse that demands your attention. This will give the interviewer just enough time to check you out. After he/she does, look back up with a friendly smile and an extended hand (when appropriate). Your interviewer will be relieved that his or her lizard brain has been placated.

## TAKING A STAND

Getting through the door, up to the stage, or to the front of the room is just the beginning. What do you do when you arrive at your destination? No matter what ActorType you are, the most effective position to stand in is the Ready Position, or what I'd like to call the Star Stance.

### The Star Stance

- Your feet are hip distance apart – (women: I'm talking hip bones, not hip flesh)
- Your body weight is slightly forward and evenly placed on the balls of both feet
- Your knees are very slightly bent
- Your arms hang loosely at your sides or are bent at the elbows, ready to gesture

The Star Stance communicates confidence and readiness. With the weight slightly forward and evenly distributed, you are ready and able to move easily in any direction. I was excited when I started taking Chi Kung classes at my gym and heard the teacher describe the Wu Chi posture. Wu Chi is a posture that many Chinese martial arts begin with and return to. As my teacher described the Wu Chi position, I realized that it is virtually the Star Stance! Then he told us one of the translations for Wu Chi, which made me even more excited. Wu Chi can be translated to mean "the emptiness from which fullness grows." When you begin in Wu Chi, the Ready Position, or in the Star Stance, you can grow and fully express anything. Your audience sees a grounded, confident, and formidable presence.

*POSTURE TABOOS*

Whereas the Star Stance or the Wu Chi posture always communicates confidence, there are postures that invite negative interpretations if used at the wrong time and/or for too long a time. The following postures may be perfectly fine to use during a casual conversation or while posing for a photo. However, when you want to gain or maintain the respect and trust of your listener, these postures should be avoided.

**Standing on one hip:**

> **Possible interpretations:** Insecure, unsteady, too casual, and, therefore, not serious about what you are speaking about.

> **Common position for:** Female Sex Symbols, Ingénues, and Buddies

**Standing with one hip slightly angled toward back of room:**

> **Possible interpretations:** This position is very subtle and easy to miss. The torso is facing front but the one hip angling back makes the listener feel that you are uncommitted; that you would rather be where that one hip is pointed – off the stage.

> **Common position for:** Curmudgeons, Whiz Kids

**Standing with crossed feet/legs:**

> **Possible interpretations:** Shy, unsteady, closed-off

Crossing any part of the body during important communication has the tendency to close you off emotionally from the person(s) you are communicating with. Standing with your legs and feet crossed while presenting at the front of the room will close you off and make you appear weaker. You have a much smaller base of balance and can easily be "pushed over." Thus you may come off to the subconscious lizard brain as a pushover.

> **Common position for:** Ingénues, some Sex Symbols

**Try this:** Stand in any one of the last three Taboo postures (standing on one hip, standing with one hip back, and standing with crossed legs or feet). Then have someone give you a push on your shoulder. You will most likely be easily pushed off balance. Then stand in the Star Stance and have someone push you, using the same exact force. You will barely budge. It's amazing how much more physically grounded you are from the Star Stance position. The reason this position is so important and so powerful is because your listener's First Brain, without actually knowing it, can assess that while you are standing in one of the taboo postures, you are less steady and literally a pushover. In the Star Stance the lizard brain recognizes that you are solid and will consequently take what you say more seriously.

**Crossing arms in front of chest:*** 

> **Possible interpretations:** Stubborn, inflexible, closed off OR hiding and insecure.

> The most common interpretation or assumption we've been told to make about crossed arms is to assume that the person is stubborn or defensive. However, exposing the torso is one of the most vulnerable postures you can assume from the stage or in front of strangers. Hiding a part of your torso is something that we instinctively do to feel less vulnerable. Crossing your arms hides a large part of your torso and therefore can more often be a sign of insecurity.

**Common position for:** Villain, Buddies, Whiz Kids

*A related position is the **Half Cross** – one arm crosses the body and holds the opposite elbow. This too is covering our torso but we fool ourselves into thinking it's okay because at least we're not crossing our arms. Wrong.

## Hands on hips:

**Possible interpretations:** Arrogant, stubborn, argumentative, aggressive, predatory

Clearly this is not a position you want to spend a lot of time in during a front-of-the-room presentation.

**Common position for:** Villains, Curmudgeons

## The "Fig Leaf":

**Possible interpretations:** Shy, protective, insecure, ashamed

As implied by the name, this position covers one of the most emotionally and physically vulnerable areas on the torso – the pelvic region. So for obvious reasons it should be avoided.

**Common position for:** Whiz Kids, Comics

## Hands in your pockets:

**Possible interpretations**: Not forthcoming, hiding something, aloof

And if you have something in your pocket, you might be tempted to fiddle with it, which will add all sorts of other distractions.

**Common position for:** Whiz Kids and Curmudgeons
*Villain ActorType is the one type that might be able to get away with this posture for a limited time.

## Hands behind your back:

**Possible interpretations:** Hiding something

This can make audience's lizard brain uncomfortable or leery. When the lizard brain watches someone whose hands are behind their back for too long, two questions may begin to form subconsciously, even if the conscious mind knows better. The lizard brain will begin to wonder: 1) What do you have behind your back? And 2) What is wrong with your hands? The illogical primitive lizard brain may even begin to wonder if you have hands.

**Common position for:** Whiz Kids, Curmudgeons, and some Super Heroes

Most of us will find ourselves slipping into one of these postures during a lengthy presentation. I am not saying that by occasionally visiting a Taboo posture you will negate all the fabulous information you are delivering. However, if you start in the Star Stance and return to it at least 75% of the time, you will leave an overall impression of someone who is trustworthy, confident, and knowledgeable.

**But what do I do with my arms? Don't worry, I will talk about arms in the Gesture section.**

Even though the Star Stance is the most powerful and effective position from which to present yourself, you do not need to plant yourself center stage and grow roots. It's perfectly fine, and often essential, for you to move across the stage or the front of the room while you are presenting. There is a huge difference, however, between purposeful movement and what many people do during a presentation when they think they are moving.

## MOVES TO LOSE

### Wandering

**What is it?** I encounter a lot of wanderers in my classes and workshops. Wanderers start in the Ready Position but in the middle of the presentation, they will begin to wander. They may believe that they are moving the way effective presenters move; however, they walk forward for several steps, then they walk back, then they walk to the side and then to the other side. They rarely stay in any spot for a full sentence and their movement has no sense of purpose – no relationship to the words or ideas they are expressing. It is difficult to make effective eye contact when you are wandering, since you are rarely in one spot for more than five seconds.

**So What?** Wandering has the effect of tiring your audience out. An audience's instinct is to follow the moving object – in this case, you. Once they discover that they can't predict where you are going to wander to next, they will begin to get tired of trying to keep up with you. Eventually, they will stop following you visually and consequently will stop listening to you.

Wandering could cause your listeners to feel that, because you have no idea where you are going physically, you may have no idea where you are going with your presentation. It makes them feel you are not organized and consequently may not know what you are talking about. If nothing else, wandering telegraphs to the listener that you are nervous.

Wandering is most common with Ingénues and Curmudgeons.

**Rockers/Swayers:**

**What is it?** Rocking and Swaying is also a common presenter habit and is very different from wandering. Swayers and Rockers think that they are standing still when they are actually shifting their weight, either forward and back or side to side – over and over and over. Most times they are not even aware they are moving. Rockers and Swayers look as though they are dancing in place with an imaginary partner.

**So what?** Rocking and Swaying is distracting because eventually your audience will not be able to focus on anything other than wondering when you are going to stop rocking. Their unconscious will make a game of trying to predict the intervals of your movement. Once you shift your weight from one foot to the other – or from one hip to the other, which is most common – the audience will feel anxious until you shift your weight again. Of course, while their minds are so creatively occupied, they will have heard little of what you had to say.

Swaying and Rocking in a familiar and steady rhythm may be a way for speakers to comfort themselves. However, the listener's instincts will correctly ascertain that if you need to comfort yourself with movement, you must be uncomfortable. And if you are uncomfortable, your audience will be uncomfortable.

Sex Symbols and some Innocents are prone to swaying.

**Fidgeters:**

**What is it?** Fidgeters differ from rockers in that they can actually stand with their feet in the ready position and manage to move every other part of their body so often and so randomly that they still give the impression of being unstable. Their knees bend and straighten, their hips go to the right then to the left, their weight shifts forward and back – all while keeping their feet firmly planted.

**So What?** Fidgeting is distracting for all the same reasons as rocking, swaying, and wandering – it makes the audience uncomfortable and makes you seem lacking in control. Fidgeting also adds a frenetic energy to the presentation, which can make your audience feel anxious. And if your audience feels anxious, they most probably will have a hard time listening or trusting what it is you are saying.

Whiz Kids and Sex Symbols are usually big fidgeters.

So now that you know the moves to lose, what are some moves you can use?

## ALL THE RIGHT MOVES

The problem with all of the above movements is that they are random and distracting, which takes away from the power of your message. Yet movement is sometimes essential. Some rooms and stages are very large and you want your whole audience to feel included, therefore moving across the stage is important. And sometimes, you have so much pent-up energy, you just have to move and that's okay.

When you feel the need to move, you can take two strong, purposeful steps going on a forward diagonal to the left or right. If that sounds overly technical, there is a reason for it. Taking just one step seems tentative and will look too much like rocking, while taking three steps can seem aggressive and too much like wandering. Also, people, even in large audiences, can be guarded about their space and taking three steps toward them can make them feel as though you are invading their territory. Moving on the diagonal just makes logical sense. If you move straight forward, you will not be reaching any more of your audience, and if you move straight to the side, half of your face and torso won't be seen.

Once you've taken two steps in one direction, hold there for a few sentences or thought groups, then take two steps in the other direction and hold there for a while. If you don't hold and speak after your two steps, your "moving" will turn into wandering.

Try to choreograph your movement to coincide with a change in your thought pattern or your topic, or use your moving to emphasize a particularly active or involving portion of your presentation – a section of your presentation that you really want your listeners to pay attention to. Taking two steps and then standing in a slightly different place might cause your listeners to think or see things slightly differently. **NOTE:** Don't panic about actually choreographing your movements. Most of us will do this type of choreography naturally if we feel connected to and passionate about what we are communicating.

Some presenters have an unconscious habit of backing up while they are talking. Walking backwards can give the audience the impression that you are backing away from them or backing down from your opinion. If you choreograph your two steps on an angle, you can usually avoid the need to back up because you will never get too far to the front of the stage. However, if you need to position yourself farther back, it is often better to turn around and walk back to where you want to be. The act of turning your back on an audience communicates that you trust them and it also gives the audience a bit of a visual break.

## Arms and Hands – Gesturing and why it's good!

One of the most common questions I get asked has to do with gesturing. To gesture or not to gesture? Most people fear that they gesture too much. Old public speaking manuals used to instruct readers to keep their hands at their side. Many "Public Speaking" teachers have continued to ascribe to that theory. However, many things have changed since the days when standing with your hands at your side was considered effective.

Good speakers use gestures to emphasize words and ideas that they feel are important; therefore when done well, gestures give your listeners visual cues to help them follow your presentation. AND NOW THERE'S A SCIENTIFIC REASON BEHIND THIS!

You may have surmised that I love all the neuroscience behind the art of public speaking, so imagine how thrilled I was when I found this information in a *Scientific American Mind* magazine about gesturing. In 2007, Jeremy Skipper of Cornell University discovered that when comprehending speech – the Broca 5 area of the brain, the part of the cortex associated with both speech production of language and gesture comprehension – appears to 'talk' to other brain regions less when the speech is accompanied by gestures. Which is to say that, when gestures are present, the Broca 5 area has an easier time processing the content of speech and may not need to draw on other brain regions to understand what is being expressed. – Scientific American Mind March/April 2010.

Translation: gestures help your listeners understand you better and enables their brains to do less work.

In nonscientific terms, gestures also add energy to the presentation. And according to Eastern philosophy, upward sweeping gestures "fluff your listeners' aura" causing them to feel better about themselves and in extension better about you and your presentation. With all these great reasons to gesture, why wouldn't you?

When you ask people why they think they should gesture less, the answer is usually because they fear that it is distracting. The truth is, anything done excessively and randomly will be distracting. Gesturing just for the sake of gesturing or because you've been told to gesture can often look wooden, repetitive, and can definitely distract your listener. Gestures are most effective when they flow naturally and are connected to the heart of what you are saying.

Many politicians and professional speakers are told that they need to gesture but are not guided on how to make those gestures look natural and congruent with their style. Therefore, what you often see are rote, robotic movements that do not flow organically from the speaker's thoughts or words, and when that happens, the incongruity of the words and gestures makes the gestures stand out and become distracting. Remember, we trust what we see more than the words we hear.

**Full disclosure:** I am a big gesturer. If you look at my videos or see me in person, you'll see that I use my hands a lot. Most of the time, I use them to emphasis points that I am making with my words. Can I do too much? Possibly. And that's where the "art" of communication comes in. Art is always going to be subjective. There may be people, depending on their experiences and preferences, who think that you gesture too much. And there may be times that you do. However, as long as you honestly feel that the gestures are connected to the heart of your material and that they are consistent with your ActorType and communication style, gesture away!

**Check it out:** Go to a full-length mirror and try to speak passionately about something you really care about without moving your arms. Not only is it difficult for most people to do, but you will see how much less engaging it is for people to watch.

The one ActorType who probably does the least amount of gesturing and can get away with it, is the Villain. Lack of gesturing makes the listener feel uncomfortable and as we see from the scientific research, forces their brains to work harder. Villains enjoy making their audience feel uncomfortable and having them work hard; therefore, limiting their gestures is an effective technique for them.

Also interesting to note is that research shows individuals who hold higher positions of power and possess larger amounts of wealth, tend to gesture less than their lower-status counterparts. This does not mean that all powerful, wealthy individuals are Villain types. And it does not mean that if you gesture, you will be considered less powerful or wealthy.

If you find that you are not a natural gesturer, don't automatically assume that you're Villain ActorType. Villains are fairly rare. What your lack of gesturing probably means is that gestures were not valued or emphasized in your public speaking experiences and you never developed or appreciated the skill. Hopefully, now you do.

## HOW TO BE A BETTER GESTURER

- Gesture from your elbows down (not just with your hands)
- Keep hands open with palms facing up
- Keep wrists loose but not limp
- Imagine that your arms and hands are extensions of your voice
- Make sure the gestures happen between your waist and your neck and move up and outwards
- Using gestures that emanate from your heart area make your words seem more connected and heartfelt. (There is a theory that gesturing from the navel area makes you seem more truthful and gesturing from the heart makes you seem more passionate.)
- Watch people who are natural gesturers and notice what they do and when
- Watch movies and see what actors in your ActorType do with their hands and arms
- Practice in front of a mirror, or on video, making gestures that are natural and not robotic

## Gestures to Lose

**Chopping motions:**

Unless you are attempting to incite a political rally or you are purposefully reprimanding someone, I would avoid using hand movements that appear to be chopping the air. These are very forceful, aggressive movements and if repeated too often, it can alienate an audience.

**Pointing:**

Think of how you feel when someone points a finger at you. Pointing looks aggressive, rude, and it usually makes you feel like you've done something wrong. Unless you want your listeners to experience those negative feelings during your communication, avoid pointing.

I've had several clients and students for whom pointing is their go-to gesture. Pointers are usually Innocents or Buddies who want to seem more authoritative and don't know how. Contrary to what you might think, pointing is not a gesture associated with the Villain type. Villains don't need to point. They are confident in their ability to influence.

**Downward palm gestures:**

The one image you need to call to mind when you think of the downward palm gesture and why you shouldn't use it is the image of Hitler and the Third Reich's salute. Look at yourself in the mirror doing a downward palm gesture and then do the same gesture with you palm facing upward. It evokes completely different feelings. People will be much more likely to respond to a request, suggestion, or statement if you say it using an upward palm rather than a downward palm.

**Fists:**

Clenching your fist while you speak or gesturing with a clenched fist are both ill-advised. You should avoid using a closed fist for the same reasons you should avoid pointing and chopping. It can look very aggressive, angry, and tight.

**Folded hands/ Interlaced Fingers:**

I went to Catholic school from the first to the eighth grade. We used to have to sit all day with our hands folded on the desk. There is obviously a reason that that gesture was used in Catholic school. Folded hands give the appearance of being attentive, submissive, and obedient. As a presenter or in any other form of communication, folding your hands could convey a similar feeling to your listeners – making them feel that you are "buttoned up," uptight, submissive, and/or holding something back.

**Below-the-waist gestures:**

I am always surprised when I see people gesture while leaving their hands down by their side. Gesturing from below-the-waist is very ineffectual and unengaging. It reminds me of a bird with an injured wing, which makes it depressing.

## GESTURES TO USE

Of course you can't gesture 100% of the time or it *would* be distracting so clients often want to know what to do with their hands when they're *not* compelled to gesture. Here are some choices:

**Palm in palm:**

Place the back of one hand inside the palm of the other. Kind of like a Mother Theresa hand gesture. This gesture isn't for everyone. It might look a little soft and be inconsistent for a Villain or a Super Hero, but it is an easy neutral resting position for other types.

**The Steeple:**

All ten finger tips touching each other and forming a steeple that either points upwards or outwards. Avoid pointing your steeple in the downward position.

This can be a very effective and comfortable resting position for your hands. It also conveys power and confidence.

*NOTE: The steeple position, though effective for most people, may, if overused by certain types, come off as arrogant and superior.

**The "Godfather"**

If you are one of those people who feel compelled to strongly emphasize thoughts and ideas, this is a gesture you can adopt that is softer and less offensive than a pointed finger but has a similar effect. I'm calling it the "Godfather" because it is the often-imitated hand gesture made famous in Italian gangster movies. Palm up with the thumb and fingers coming together to form an "O" when you look at the hand from the side. You can use this gesture to point or for other emphasis.

**The "OK" point**

Instead of pointing that index finger, let it touch your thumb creating the "OK" gesture. You can use this hand position to gesture palm up or palm facing out.

**Relaxed open palm:**

This is the simplest and most neutral of gestures. Showing your palms communicates trust to the lizard brain of your listener – probably derived from the simple fact that an open palm carries no weapon. Therefore, gesturing with your relaxed open, upward-facing palm is one of the most effective types of gesture you can use.

# THE WARDROBE DEPARTMENT

Clothes make the man (and woman) and, of course, what you wear greatly impacts people's first impression of you. There are many wonderful books written about styling and dressing. However, this is not one of them. So I will not go into a lot of detail about what you should and shouldn't wear, but I do have some tips about how to find a style that's right for your type.

There are two important factors to think about when dressing for a presentation, interview, or any other professional event: make sure your style is 1) appropriate for your audience and your body type and 2) is consistent with your personality and ActorType. For example: If you are a Hero, Innocent, or Super Hero addressing a corporate crowd, it would be less effective for you to show up in business casual. However, a Whiz Kid or a Curmudgeon when addressing the same crowd could wear more casual clothing and still be effective.

## APPROPRIATENESS

Many books and advice givers will still tell all job applicants to wear a black or blue suit. But what if you are interviewing for a job at a dot-com or at a public relations firm? Wearing a suit might cause you to come off as too buttoned-up, stuffy and boring. Being overdressed can also lessen your effectiveness by putting up a distracting "barrier" between you and your audience.

Think of all the scenes in films or television where a character enters a room and all eyes turn because he or she is wearing something hopelessly inappropriate. In the 2011 film *The Help*, the character Celia enters a party in a skin-tight overly sexy gown when everyone else is wearing southern party dresses. It's obvious from the moment she walks in that she will not have a successful evening. You don't want that to happen to you.

In almost every popular magazine these days, pages and pages are devoted to what stars are wearing and whether or not what they are wearing is appropriate.

But how do we know what's appropriate when superstars with personal stylists can't seem to get it right? Here is what I suggest if you are presenting or interviewing at an unknown venue: Research the company that you are interviewing with or presenting to and find out the typical dress code or style. You can find out the dress code in a couple of different ways. If you have time, and if it is logistically possible, you could visit, or have someone you know visit, the place of business a few days before and observe how people are dressing. If you are doing a presentation, it is common and advised to ask if you can stop by in advance to see the space. This is a perfect opportunity to observe the dress code. Another easier way to assess the style and fashion culture of a business is simply to ask. You can call the receptionist or your contact person and ask about the typical dress code. You don't even need to identify yourself to the receptionist. Once you've done your research, you should plan to dress one level above how the majority of the people dress at the venue where you'll be presenting or interviewing. For example, if the majority of people show up in business casual … it would be appropriate for you to show up in a suit. If there are a number of people in jeans or other casual wear, business casual would be suitable. If it's a corporate everyone-in-suits culture, time to break out the nicest suit in your wardrobe.

Dressing one notch above also goes for speaking in front of an audience of your peers and colleagues. If you're presenting at a meeting or conference, on presentation day, instead of wearing your usual attire, choose something that's a tad more put together and polished. Even though they may see you every day, if you are sharing information from the front of the room, you want to look and feel more polished.

## Consistency

In films like *Pygmalion*, *Pretty Woman*, and countless others, there's always the exciting scene when the star is taken on a shopping spree and finally gets clothes that are consistent with the incredible person who's been hidden under the wrong outfits.

Many of us are guilty of a similar offense. We are wearing clothing that is inconsistent with the incredible people we are. We dress in ways that may reflect what we think we should wear, what we've always worn, or what other people are wearing. True Super Stars find a signature style that communicates something about who they are and what they have to give without seeming inappropriate.

When a costume designers get hired to work on a movie, TV show, or play, one of the first things that they do is research. They research the character's personality; what the director wants the audience to think/feel about the character's economic background, taste level, occupation, and lifestyle. The exercises on the next page are created to help you get started on your own costume design research.

## DRESSING YOUR TYPE

1) Look over the following list of positive adjectives. How would you describe yourself and your business? (Bonus: You can also use this list to read through as a subliminal confidence booster!)

## POSITIVE PERSONALITY ADJECTIVES

| | | | | |
|---|---|---|---|---|
| alluring | diligent | generous | peaceful | successful |
| ambitious | discreet | gentle | perfect | succinct |
| amused | dynamic | glorious | plausible | talented |
| boundless | eager | happy | pleasant | thoughtful |

| | | | | |
|---|---|---|---|---|
| brave | edgy | harmonious | plucky | thrifty |
| bright | efficient | helpful | productive | tough |
| calm | elated | hilarious | proud quiet | trustworthy |
| capable | eminent | honorable | receptive | unbiased |
| charming | enchanting | impartial | reflective | unusual |
| cheerful | encouraging | industrious | responsible | upbeat |
| comfortable | endurable | instinctive | righteous | vigorous |
| confident | energetic | jolly | romantic | vivacious |
| cooperative | entertaining | joyous kind | sedate | warm |
| courageous | enthusiastic | kind-hearted | selective | willing |
| credible | excellent | knowledge-able | self-assured | wise |
| cultured | excited | level | sensitive | witty |
| dashing | exclusive | likeable | shrewd | wonderful |
| dazzling | exuberant | lively | silly | |
| debonair | fabulous | lovely | sincere | |
| decisive | fantastic | loving | skillful | |
| decorous | fearless | lucky | smiling | |
| delightful | frank | mature | splendid | |
| detailed | friendly | modern | steadfast | |
| determined | funny | painstaking | stimulating | |

Ask a close friend or colleague to look over the list, or use social media to reach out to your fans.

What five words would they use to describe you?

1) Now look back at the values that describe your ActorType.

2) Write down all the adjectives that you've gathered so far.

3) With that list in hand (or in mind) spend some time doing research. Look at magazines, television shows, people around your office, or on the street. Make a physical or mental note every time you see someone wearing something that seems to communicate one of your adjectives. Rip out images from magazines. Take a picture, whenever possible, of any image that speaks to your style. In this world of camera phones and iPads that shouldn't be hard.

4) Now go over your list of adjectives, your research list, and any images you've collected; write down any specific colors, textures, and styles that resonate with you and your adjectives.

5) Check out your closet to see how many "if any" of those styles, colors, textures etc. you already possess.

6) THE FUN PART: Go out and buy at least FIVE items that really represent the qualities on your list. These could be a scarf, a tie, a piece of jewelry, an entire outfit, colorful shoes, or serious conservative shoes.

After doing this exercise, if you still feel that dressing for your ActorType, body type, or profession is more than you can handle, there is always help available. Check out Appendix I for a list of stylists, blogs, and websites I recommend.

# ZOOMING IN

So we have our Establishing Shot in the can. You're dressed appropriately and consistently with your ActorType; you know how to stand, move, and gesture to be consistent with your type and not distract from your message. Now the camera begins to zoom in.

*ARE YOU READY FOR YOUR CLOSE-UP?*

Without "close-ups" in movies or television, it would be difficult for viewers to emotionally relate to what a character is feeling or experiencing. The close-up is designed to help viewers understand and/ or connect with characters whom the director feels are important to understand and empathize with. As speakers, you want your viewers to connect with and understand you as well. So when your audience zooms in on you, you want to be sure you're ready for your close-up. Let's look at what goes into creating an effective close-up.

## THE EYES HAVE IT – EYE CONTACT AND HOW TO USE IT

Effective eye communication is the most important skill a presenter can master. Everyone seems to know this intellectually, so why does it seem so hard to put into effect once we get in the front of the room or across from an interviewer?

"The eyes are the window to the soul." I believe some people have a basic fear of eye contact because they either don't wish to see into the other person's soul or don't feel comfortable having the other person see into theirs. However, without sustained eye contact, real, effective communication is usually not taking place*. It's important to note that by sustained eye contact, I don't mean staring. Your mother was right, staring is rude. Sustained eye contact, however is the opposite of rude.

**\*Soap Box**

When I talk about eye contact, someone will inevitably mention that in certain cultures any eye contact is considered rude. Yes, there are cultural differences. Here's the thing: this book is written by an American and is meant to be helpful to individuals interacting with people within, or comfortable with, cultural norms accepted in the United States. I have taught individuals from many different cultures over the past 15 years. What I share with them and what I share within the pages of this book is what is most effective in this culture. For people who want to be more effective communicating in this country and in this culture, using the information I am sharing is one way of improving their effectiveness. I have no expertise in judging or assessing what people in other cultures find effective. There are several other books that do address cultural differences. My personal opinion is that just as English is becoming an international language, the nonverbal language described in this book may also be on its way to becoming universally accepted. Scorcese fans may not appreciate Tarantino movies and vice versa. However, both directors get their messages across. Communication is an art and is therefore always going to be subjective.

THE 5-10-SECOND RULE

A rule of thumb to remember is the 5-10-second rule. Maintain eye contact with an individual for at least 5 seconds and no longer than 10 seconds before looking away briefly. If you make eye contact for less than 5 seconds, you risk appearing "shifty-eyed," which can convey insecurity, insincerity, and dishonesty. You've all seen those movies where the guilty party has an impossible time looking his or her accuser in the eye.

On the other hand, there can be too much of a good thing. Eye contact sustained for too long without a break will make the other person feel uncomfortable. If you maintain eye contact for more than 10 seconds, you run the risk of seeming as though you want to either get intimate with the person you're staring at, or you are trying to intimidate them. Unless you really want to date or scare the person with whom you are talking, it's important to keep your eye contact within the appropriate length of time.

If you're thinking, "I don't want to be counting seconds off in my head while I'm speaking to someone," you can use another rule of thumb.

### THE HOLD (FOR) THAT THOUGHT RULE

Maintain eye contact for an entire sentence or thought group before you look away. This works well unless you are one of those people who likes to string thoughts and sentences together, or are someone who speaks in very short sentences.

**Villains** and **Sex Symbols** will often go over the 10-second limit, while Whiz Kids and Curmudgeons tend to err on the other side – going under 5 seconds. If you are one of these types, it's important to get conscious of what your eyes are doing and practice one of these two rules of thumb.

## GIVE US A BREAK!

Breaking eye contact is important, not just for the other person's comfort level but because it gives your listener a chance to let his or her eyes have a break too. This actually allows your listener's to access different parts of the brain, allowing them to store and sort through the information you are sharing. It also will allow them to access information they need in order to answer your questions or comment on what you have just said. Most people's eyes will travel in one direction when they are creating visual information, (to their right) and another direction when they are pulling out visual memories (to their left). The eyes travel in other directions when we access sounds and emotions and still another when we are having an internal dialogue.

So with all the work the eyes and the brain are doing, you can see how locking eyes with your listener could hinder complete communication.

**Try it out:**

Have a casual conversation with someone and do not break eye contact, not even for a nanosecond. Ask them how that made them feel. Then switch and see how it makes you feel. Whenever I do this in a workshop or presentation, the person either will inevitably tell me they felt that I wanted to date them, or will give me a nonverbal response that means that I "creeped them out."

Eye contact at meetings and from the front of the room is just as important as eye contact during one-on-one communication. Many of the same concepts apply.

### GROUP AND FRONT-OF-THE-ROOM EYE CONTACT

There used to be people who taught speakers to look over the audience's heads during a presentation. I have had clients who still thought that was an okay technique to use. It's not! Hopefully no one teaches that any more. The 5-10-second and the hold-that-thought rules of eye contact also apply when you are speaking to a group or a large audience – you just have a lot more sets of eyes to make contact with.

The most important part of making eye contact from the front of the room or at a meeting is to make everyone feel as though you are including them in your presentation or conversation no matter how many of them there are. Looking above their heads does not make an audience feel included; it makes them feel incidental. Of course, you may not be able to look at each and every person in your audience, but you can make them feel as though you are. The best way you accomplish this is to make 5-10-second eye contact with one person in one section of the room at a time. When you give sincere eye contact to one person in one section of the room, the people within a few feet of that person will feel "taken care of." Each person in that section may even think you are looking at him/her. (We all know how difficult it is to tell when someone from the front of the room is really looking at us. How many times have you been in an audience when the person on stage calls on you and you wonder if they are talking to you or the person behind you?)

When you have made 5-10 seconds-worth of eye contact or have delivered a complete sentence or thought group to that one person in that one section of the room, move to another person in a completely different section of the room. That entire section will then feel your attention on them. Continue doing this throughout your presentation or meeting. You do not have to worry about any logical order. Go from front right, to back left, to middle right to far back. It's best to randomly select different people in each section each time you go back to that section. This will keep the entire audience engaged. Added bonus is they won't know where your gaze will fall next, which causes them pay closer attention. And don't forget to occasionally direct your attention to those people who like to sit alone or off to the sides of the room.

## Spread the Love

Many people at meetings or when making presentations will make the mistake of getting sucked into some magnetic pull that causes them to focus their eye contact primarily or completely on one person or on one side of the room. This is problematic for two reasons:

1)   The people with whom you are not making eye contact are going to start feeling alienated and ignored. They will begin to feel as though your information or message is not for them. This gives them permission and the opportunity to let their minds wander and/or their electronic devices beckon. If they get the impression that you don't care about their being in the room, they will find something in cyberspace or their own minds to occupy their time.

2.   The recipients of your exclusive eye contact will begin to feel uncomfortable and embarrassed. If you continually make eye contact and direct your attention to the same person, that person is acutely aware of the fact that you are neglecting others at their expense. They also long to be released from having to respond and react to every word coming out of your mouth. Depending on their sense of self, they may begin to feel that you "like" them too much or that you're judging them and thinking they are the only ones who really need to hear what it is you are saying. These feelings will also

be felt if you are favoring one *side* of the room over the other. Each person on the side that you are favoring will most likely notice that you are not paying attention to the other side and will eventually begin to empathize and feel sorry for the neglected side of the room.

You can imagine that with all this drama going on in people's minds, there is precious little time for them to take in what it is you are actually talking about. Since, presumably, the purpose of your presentation is to reach and affect as many people as possible, be sure to distribute your eye contact evenly and fairly.

Special note to salespeople who deal with couples: In my work with financial advisors, I am constantly amazed at how often advisors will favor one sex over the other. No surprise that the husband usually gets the majority of the eye contact. I have been in role-playing meetings where I got 20% of the eye contact. When that happens, I feel like I'm watching the meeting take place on television and I wish I could change the channel. I have an impossible time making sense of what is being said. My thoughts turn instead to how much I want to get out of there and how I would never want to take another meeting with this person again. Needless to say, an experience like that would cost the advisor a couple's business.

**Eye contact Tips and Tricks:**

- If you know you have trouble sustaining eye contact, here's a tip: You do not need to look directly into a person's eyes.

If you look somewhere in the center of the face (one eye, the nose, between the eyes) Taking the above tip a step further, if a person intimidates you and looking into their eyes makes your knees shake, look at their forehead – right between the eyes. This way it looks as though you are courageously making eye contact, but by having your gaze above their eye line you are less likely to be emotionally affected by what they are saying. Great trick for receiving performance reviews.

- There is a difference between eye contact and looking. Sometimes your eyes are focused on a person, but your mind is elsewhere so you look like you're looking through them. People can feel the difference. Really try to make a connection and share something with the person you have decided to make eye contact with.

**Two More Important Reasons to Make Eye Contact**

1) Contrary to what you might think, making eye contact does not make you more nervous. Instead, making eye contact actually "grounds" you and gives you more energy. It can be wonderfully energizing to connect with another human being who is interested in what you have to say. And for those of you who are now thinking, "But what if they aren't interested in what I have to say," that leads to the second-most-important reason to make eye contact.

2)     Eye Contact allows you to assess your audience. If you see the majority of your audience glazed over or busying themselves with other things, that's an important cue for you to inject your presentation with some audience involvement techniques. I will go over some specifics in the following chapter.

## FACE FACTS – Facial Expressions: Make Them Work for You, Not Against You

There are more than 40 muscles in the human face that enable us to make thousands of different facial expressions. The interpretation of these expressions is a continual field of study for scientists.

Successful poker players are usually very skilled at learning to read their opponents' "tells" – the tiny facial expressions players display that "tell" whether they have a good hand or a bad one.

Similarly, during a communication, if you are feeling insecure, nervous, worried, or doubtful, your facial expressions can betray you. That betrayal can happen in a millisecond. The listeners may not have worked on honing their face-reading skills like poker players and may not be able to identify the exact facial muscle combinations that make your words less believable, but, on a subconscious level they will still feel that your facial expressions are not consistent with the words you are saying. Again, as I stated earlier, when given a choice between believing what we see over

what we hear, people will almost always believe what they see –
your facial expressions – over what they hear – your words.

Many people have habitual or default facial expressions that they
may not be aware of. I'm sure you have met people who look as
though they are always worried, angry, or frightened. There are
even people who always look happy even when they're not. The
muscles of their faces have formed these expressions so often that
the expression becomes their "normal."

That is why videotape can be your best friend. I videotape all of
my clients' sessions and many of them are amazed to discover that
they have "default" expressions or habitual facial tells.

I was recently working with a client who had just begun a new job
as a manager and team leader in a large corporation. She came to
me because, having been out of work for quite a while, she was
insecure about her leadership communication style. We worked
on finding her assertiveness through her voice, body language,
and word choice. Then, during one session, we were role-playing
a meeting where she had to express a strong opinion. As we
looked back at the videotape, she noticed that her face looked
insecure whenever she expressed a strong opinion. Specifically,
she would raise her eyebrows and open her eyes very wide. This
is an expression of innocence and vulnerability. The opposite of
what she was trying to convey. The solution was not to consciously
think of not raising her eyebrows. It is difficult to concentrate on
NOT doing something. It is much more effective to concentrate

on DOING something else. In this instance, seeing how the insecurity was leaking out in her expression allowed us to address the insecurity itself. This particular person was a Buddy/Innocent ActorType by default and cared a lot about being liked. But she also had a lot of Whiz Kid in her, which, gave her a lot of wisdom and ability to get things done. In this case, I worked on elevating her Whiz Kid traits by convincing her that the points she needed to express were very important to her audience. This way we were able to reframe her purpose for expressing her opinion. Instead of worrying about how she would be judged for her opinion, I helped her to understand that she was actually helping people by expressing her opinion. By bringing the tell into her awareness and changing her intent and her purpose behind the communication, the "insecure" facial tell disappeared.

One of the only ways to find out if you have a default facial expression that interferes with your communication's effectiveness is to get honest feedback either from a coach or from the most honest feedback mechanism of all: video. A good idea might be to tape yourself while you're on the phone having an actual conversation so that you can see what your face does naturally. You can also ask a colleague to tape you during one of your presentations.

Once you discover any physical tick, habit, or emotional tell, there are two ways that you can work on it: You can work on it from the outside, in – consciously bring awareness to whatever habit you have and then try to replace that habit with a more effective habit. Or you can work on changing the habit from the inside, out

– try to discover what feelings are coming up for you when you are making that particular expression and learn to replace those feelings with feelings that will be more useful and consistent with the communication you would like to deliver. Or you can do both at once.

**You're Never Fully Dressed Without Your...**

Whatever your default expression may be, the most effective and universally understood facial expression is the smile. Nothing can put an audience at ease like a genuine and appropriate smile.

"Appropriate" is the operative word here. Many of my clients tell me that they feel they can't smile because the subject is serious and they don't want to appear foolish or insensitive. I understand the argument. When we think of smiling, we tend to think of a broad toothy grin, but there are many variations on the smile. You might not want to let loose a broad grin when you're about to fire someone. In that type of situation, you probably would not want to smile at all.

However, for a front-of-the-room presentation or when chairing meetings, a smile is important. Your smile makes you appear more engaging and approachable. It is also a way to put your listeners at ease. Smiling affects a part of the viewers' brains that encourages them to smile back. Albeit there are definitely times in the work place when a more serious face, or even a poker face, is called for. I wholeheartedly believe that you can adopt an appropriate smile for most situations. Sometimes a closed-mouth smile or a half smile will be more appropriate. Sometimes a warm open or closed-mouth smile will be what the occasion needs to put people at ease. The way you smile will not only be dictated by the situation, but may also be dictated by your dominant ActorType.

If you lean towards the Villain ActorType, you may choose to greet your audience with a deadpan stare and eventually (and I strongly suggest that you do) let a sly smile escape. The Villains' lack of smile is often part of their charm and charisma. However, for Curmudgeons and Whiz Kids, who are typically smile challenged, their lack of a smile does not come across as charming or charismatic and can be perceived as cranky, mean, or distant.

My advice for Curmudgeons, Whiz Kids, and those who are not natural smilers is – practice makes perfect. Many body builders had no calf definition before they devoted themselves to exercising their calf muscles. As relationship builders we need to spend some time developing our zygomatic major and orbicularis oculi muscles – the two sets of muscles that make up a genuine smile.

- Spend some time in front of a mirror or a video camera and exercise your smile muscles until smiling comes to you more naturally.
- Make sure you are not just smiling with your mouth. The orbicularis oculi are the muscles around your eyes that need to engage in order to make your smile look genuine.

- Make a conscious decision to smile at a minimum of three to five people a day. It's okay to practice with strangers who don't know you for the poker face that you used to be.
- You will probably start noticing that presentations and encounters are more engaging and more positively received. You'll also be amazed at how much happier you will become. Studies have shown that the physical act of smiling alone, even if you aren't feeling particularly happy, will raise your level of feel-good hormones and you will begin to feel happier.

## TOO MUCH OF A GOOD THING

Alas, sometimes even smiling can be too much of a good thing. There are some people for whom a smile is the default expression. Innocents and Sex Symbols are often guilty of this habit. Smiling too much can be almost as problematic as not smiling enough. As positive and infectious as a smile is, if you smile too often or too indiscriminately, listeners may begin to think of you as shallow or insincere. Often people will use a smile as a default expression to mask insecurity or nervousness. Your lizard brain knows that when a person sees you smile, they will feel more comfortable or trusting of you so when your insecurities run amok, the lizard brain tries to protect you, by smiling. Use videotaping and self-observation to become aware of whether or not you are an over-smiler.

**THE BOTTOM LINE:** Using videotape or coaching feedback will help you find out if your facial expressions are undermining your communication. However, one of the surest ways to eliminate distracting facial expressions is to be sure to stay truly connected to your listener and the information you are hearing and sharing. When you stay present and attentive as a listener and maintain a passion for and/or connection to your message, there is a better chance that your facial expressions will be authentic and appropriate.

# VOICE AND VOCAL TONE – YOUR SOUND TRACK

From Mehrabian's study, we learned that Vocal communication accounts for 38% of your message during an in-person communication. Over the phone, the tone of your voice makes up **84%** of your message's effectiveness. With the tone of your voice having that much importance, improving your vocal quality is essential to improving your communication skills.

The birth of the talkies is the basis for the movies *Singin in the Rain* and *The Artist.* Both movies illustrate how with the birth of talkies many Hollywood actors became unemployable. Why? Because Hollywood knew all too well how much gets communicated through the tone of the voice. Hollywood knew that certain stars would not be as credible or likeable to audiences once audiences heard the actors speak.

## WHAT IS VOCAL TONE?

When we talk about vocal quality or tone we're talking about:

- **Volume** – Is it too loud or too soft?
- **Resonance** – Is there a rich, full tone to the voice? Or Is it thin and tinny?
- **Pitch** – Is it deep with low tones like Barry White's, or higher pitched?

- **Articulation** – Are the individual sounds clearly pronounced or are they soft and mushed together?
- **Intonation** – Is there variety in the tones or does every word come out with the same tonality – monotone? This is also where accent, regionalisms, and dialects come into play.
- **Pace** – Do the words tumble out quickly or do they come out very slowly?

A combination of all these qualities makes up your vocal tone. When one of these factors becomes distracting to your listener, you run the risk of losing credibility and/or likeability, just as like some silent film stars did. Although it's commonly said that the eyes are the windows to the soul, I once heard someone state the voice is the window of the heart. I love that thought. I find it to be very true. The depth of your character, the strength of your convictions, and the connectedness to your purpose can all be communicated through the tone of your voice.

## TUNING UP YOUR TONE

Improving your vocal tone can be just as important as improving your muscle tone. It can also require just as much work. Despite what they tell you on infomercials, if you want to build healthy strong muscles, there is no magic bullet. Going from flabby to buff requires hours of consistently doing strenuous, repetitive exercises. Changing your vocal tone requires the same amount of consistency and dedication. But it can be done. I know, because

I did it. As a child, as if being called "Shai" wasn't bad enough, I was also told that I had a "cute" high-pitched voice. My family called it a "fry" voice. I have no idea where that came from. At the risk of outing my family's political incorrectness, they also used to say I had a "Chinese" voice. With the acting I did in high school, my voice had taken on a slightly deeper tone. But it was when I went to college and majored in theatre that my voice was really given a workout. As a theatre major, I had mandatory voice and diction classes three times a week at eight o'clock in the morning for four years. We did drills and exercises targeting each of the six elements that I listed above. After four years of training, it is safe to say that my voice is no longer cute or high pitched. I am happy to report that my voice is now often the first thing people notice and remember about me. I've also done radio commercials and film voice work based on the quality of my voice.

I know firsthand that having a strong, clear, powerful voice is a surefire way to get and hold people's attention. It is unbelievable how many times I have been able to get my point across during noisy, chaotic meetings or meandering discussions purely by using the power of my voice.

So what did I learn in my early-morning voice and diction classes that turned my "fry" voice into a power voice? The first and most important thing I learned was how to speak from the diaphragm.

The **diaphragm** is a sheet of muscle extending across the bottom of your rib cage. In order to produce and support a strong, powerful voice, the diaphragm muscle needs to be strong and flexible. Most women bypass their diaphragms and use their throat muscles and vocal chords to produce sound. This often leads to the higher-pitched, thinner sounds that many women have. Men are better at engaging their diaphragms for reasons I have yet to discover, but men also can benefit from strengthening this muscle so that their voices are supported, full, and easily projected.

I always knew how important speaking from the diaphragm was, and for years talked about how using your diaphragm during long presentations keeps you from hurting your throat. Then I was given the "opportunity" to put my diaphragm to the test. The day before a big presentation, I felt a chest cold settling in. By midafternoon, I had a full-blown case of laryngitis. My throat was infected and it was very difficult to speak. I ran to the store and bought every medication I could find and rested my voice for the rest of the night. The next morning, it still wasn't great; the infection still made my voice very tight sounding and full of cracks and breaks. Since it was not possible to cancel or postpone the presentation, I went in anyway. When it was time to present, instead of using my throat, I used my stomach muscles to push breath through my diaphragm to produce a resonant, though very husky, sound. I got through the whole presentation without having to tax my infected vocal cords. That day taught me exactly just how important having a strong diaphragm is.

Below are some of the breathing exercises designed to engage and strengthen the diaphragm muscle. But just as reading about sit-ups won't get you a six-pack, reading about strengthening your diaphragm won't improve your tone. It's important for you to work on these exercises at least two to three times a week. To hear examples of the exercises and for a complete guided vocal workout, pick up a copy of my *Vocal Workout* CD, available on Amazon.com and on my website: www.Speaketc.com

DIAPHRAGMATIC BREATHING:

This is a basic breathing exercise very similar to breathing exercises in yoga, meditation, or pilates.

Do this exercise in front of a mirror so that you can see your rib cage expanding.

- Place your hands around your lower rib cage, thumbs hugging the back ribs, fingers pointing towards the front.
- Inhale deeply through your nose, filling your belly first then your chest.
- Feel your ribcage push against your hands as it expands. This is caused by your diaphragm muscle expanding and dropping as the air pushes against it. If you are in front of a mirror, you should be able to see your hands move away from each other.
- Your shoulders should not rise when you breathe in. If you notice your shoulders up by your ears, you're holding on to too much tension. Breathe out and try it again and think of the air expanding, not lifting.
- Now exhale letting the air out very slowly. Keeping your hands on your rib cage, make sure it remains expanded until all the

air has been released. Watch your hands and make sure they remain separated.

- When all the air has been released, collapse your ribcage and then breathe in again.
- Repeat several times until it feels easy to breathe this way.

DIAPHRAGM PUSH-UPS:

This exercise strengthens your diaphragm muscle so that it can better support your breath and produce richer, stronger tones. This is especially helpful for women who want to add resonance and richness to their voices and for men who want to sound stronger and more confident.

- Place two of your fingers in the center of your rib cage. You should feel a soft indentation.
- Repeat the above breathing exercise, but instead of slowly letting the air out, pull your stomach muscles in to press the air up through your diaphragm and let out a series of short "ha" sounds. This should be a staccato sound that feels like it is coming from the center of your chest. You should not experience any throat tension as you make this sound.
- As you let out the short staccato "ha" sounds, you should be able to feel a muscle moving in and out through the soft indentation in your chest. That is your diaphragm muscle in action.
- If you are not sure if you are getting the right sound, try letting out a deep sigh. When we let out a deep sigh, the sound that

escapes is usually produced by your diaphragm. Once you feel the vibration that happens in your diaphragm when you sigh, go back and try to do the exercise from that place.

- Do several sets of diaphragm push-ups daily and I guarantee that you will begin to notice a richer tone to your voice.

### VOLUME / PROJECTION

It's infuriating to sit through a lecture or presentation and not be able to hear the speaker clearly. If you've ever been in that situation, I'm sure you have observed or have even been the lone audience member who chooses to address the situation. "SPEAK UP!" they shout, as if the speaker has committed a personal affront. And "in fact," he has. Audience members have many other things to do besides attend your meeting or presentation. It can feel disrespectful and insulting if the speaker uses a volume that carries only to the front two rows. Be cognizant of the fact that when you are doing a presentation or speaking at a meeting, you should not speak at the same volume as you would during a personal, one-on-one conversation. There needs to be a different energy and part of that energy should be achieved by using a slightly raised volume. I am not suggesting you yell or strain your voice. The most effective way to raise your volume and produce the additional energy you need for meetings or presentations is to speak from your diaphragm and not your throat.

If you've done the above exercises, you will now be able to locate, activate, and strengthen your diaphragm muscle. Try the following exercise to practice using your newfound diaphragm to project your voice over longer distances without straining your throat or vocal chords.

## PROJECTION PRACTICE

**Caution: You might want to do the following exercises when home alone.**

- Take a breath using diaphragmatic breathing; instead of exhaling, say the sentence: *"We have exceeded our goal for the quarter"* (or any other line you choose).
- Now, repeat the phrase as if you are speaking from a stage to a large crowd 20-30 feet in front of you. Really visualize your voice shooting out and hitting a wall in the far distance. If you happen to be in a tiny room, face a window and imagine your voice shooting into the building next door or across the street.
- Make sure the sound is coming from the diaphragm and not the throat. You should be able to feel the difference based on the amount of tension in your neck and throat. If you feel strain or tension, you are using your throat muscles and not your diaphragm. Keep trying until you can feel the difference.
- When you think you've spoken as loudly as possible, try to go one decibel louder. I'm sure you have it in you!

**During a Presentation:**

Imagine sending your voice to the last person in the last row. Your goal, with any presentation, should be to affect everyone within ear shot. If you put your attention to making sure the last row hears you, your projection will most likely be adequate. It is rare that an audience complains about a speaker being too loud. In the rare cases that this happens, the complaint is usually based on the fact that the speaker has limited vocal variety and/or resonance, so the audience feels as though they are being shouted at.

And remember, presentations should be two-way streets. If you don't know whether you are being heard or whether you are speaking too loudly – ASK!

*WHAT IF I'M USING A MICROPHONE?*

It's difficult to give general advice for microphone use as there are hundreds of different types of microphones. Hand-held, body mike (lavaliere), standing mike, directional mike …

If you are going to be using a microphone, see if you can get an opportunity to test the equipment beforehand. Some are extremely sensitive. You can practically whisper in the direction of the microphone and be heard. With others, you have to speak directly into the "live" part of it or your voice will not be amplified. Most venues will have a sound technician working with the presenters, so get to your presentation early enough to ask him or her how "live" the microphone is. They will probably be sure to test you for "levels" before you begin.

If there is no technician and/or you are not able to practice with the equipment beforehand, be sure to check in with your audience before you launch into your presentation. Ask the audience if they can hear you and make adjustments accordingly.

Microphone or no microphone, you still need to speak from your diaphragm. Using your diaphragm muscles protects your throat from overuse and abuse, and creates a much more resonant, powerful, and pleasant sound.

## VOCAL RESONANCE

*Res o nance (noun) Ringing quality of instrument or voice: an amplification of a sound, e.g. that of an instrument or the human voice, caused by sympathetic vibration in a chamber such as an auditorium or a singer's chest. (ENCARTA DICTIONARY)*

When we talk about vocal resonance for speaking, we are talking about the sound or amplification of your voice as it vibrates in three different areas of your body: the chest, the nose, and the facial mask (the area behind your face).

When you hear voices that sound thin, shrill, or nasal it is because the vocal sound is vibrating primarily in only one or two of the three areas. In order to have an interesting resonant voice, it is important to learn how to make sound vibrate in all three of your vocal resonators.

## RESONANCE EXERCISE

The following exercise provoked a lot of laughter and resistance when I first learned it in college, but my thin, high-pitched voice quickly morphed into the resonant voice I have today, therefore I no longer make fun of this exercise and use it regularly with my clients. It is designed to activate and warm up all three of the vocal resonators.

- Take a deep diaphragmatic breath in.
- Place your hands on either side of your nose and repeat the sound "NEE" pushing the air towards your nasal cavity.

"NEE, NEE, NEE"
Feel your nasal cavity vibrate?

- Now move your hands to just underneath your chin and repeat the sound "NOO":

"NOO NOO NOO"

- Feel for the vibration of your vocal folds, which should vibrate within the entire facial mask.

- Next place your hands on your chest and say "NAH"

"NAH, NAH, NAH!"

You should feel your chest vibrate. The goal is to produce a full, rich sound from your chest and diaphragm. Make sure your throat is relaxed with no strain or tension.

Repeat this exercise going up and down in pitch to add variety to your tone. For a full and resonant voice, it is important to activate all of these resonators when you speak. By doing this exercise, you can strengthen and activate the resonators that are weak.

## THE RAIN IN SPAIN – ARTICULATION AND PRONUNCIATION

Having a strong, resonant voice is only half the battle. You still have to be able to pronounce words so that people can easily understand them.

To fully metamorphose from ugly duckling to swan, Eliza Doolittle *(My Fair Lady)*, Bille Dawn *(Born Yesterday)*, and many other movie heroines are subjected to hours of grueling articulation exercises. And let's not leave out our one movie star male Hero: Colin Firth *(The King's Speech)*. In the above examples, our heroines (and *lone hero*) also had accents, speech impediments, and dialects to overcome. However, many native speakers with no discernible dialect, accent, or impediment are still difficult to understand because of poor articulation.

Poor articulation can often be attributed to weakness, underdevelopment, or laziness in the muscles of the **lips** and the **tongue**. Yes, they have muscles too! These muscles need to be toned in order to do their jobs effectively. And just like arms, legs, and diaphragms, the tongue and the lip muscles can get stronger with exercise. My first year in pronunciation classes, I was accused of having a "lazy tongue." I am not making this up. My family already had told me I had a high-pitched voice and here my diction teacher tells me I have a lazy tongue. I was able to whip my lazy tongue into shape through some of the following exercises.

## The Warm-Up

### Horse Flutters – AKA Giving the Raspberry

- Take a deep breath.
- Force air through your lips making a "BRRR" sound.
- Let the sound vibrate energy to your lips.
- Go up and down in pitch to add musicality.

### Tongue Flutters – AKA Spanish "R"

- Roll the tongue, vibrating it against the alveolar ridge making an "r" sound.
- Go up and down in pitch.

I realize that, genetically, some people aren't able to do this. If you are one of them, skip to the next exercise.

## THE WORK-OUT

Now that your tongue and lips are warmed up, let's put them to work. Below is a series of Articulation Drills. These drills are designed to engage the muscles of your lips, tongue, and mouth that are involved in making challenging vowel and consonant combinations.

You may find some more difficult than others. The degree of difficulty will vary depending on where you were raised and what pronunciation habits you have developed. Regardless of whether or not you find a drill challenging, it is a good idea to work on all of the sentences in order to strengthen and tone your instrument.

My personal favorite, and most universally helpful drill is:

"THE TEETH, THE LIPS, THE TIP OF THE TONGUE."

If you don't do any other of the drills regularly, you should use this drill before you have to give a speech or presentation.

To get the most out of this exercise and all the exercises to follow, it is important to overly exaggerate the formation of the sounds. For example, to make the "T" sound, the tip of your tongue should tense and touch the ridge right behind your top teeth with a force strong enough to move the flame of a candle.

For the "th" sound make sure the tip of the tongue is forcefully pushing air between the teeth.

Also work the final "P." The letter P (along with the letters K and T) is called a plosive. Make sure it explodes with a burst of air.

Of course, in normal speech, I'm not advising you to exaggerate like I'm suggesting here, but this is a workout. We lift 10-pound weights at the gym to prepare us to lift five-pound bags of groceries.

Once you feel comfortable clearly and precisely articulating this sentence, work on seeing how quickly you can repeat it 10 times in a row, with the same precision and clarity.

*MORE ARTICULATION DRILLS:*

Below are a few more challenging sentences to practice with. Be sure to exaggerate each sound and finish each word. I've listed the consonant combinations that are being targeted in each sentence, but make sure to clearly articulate even the nontargeted consonants.

(SH, S)
If you wish to speak clearly just practice sincerely
Sally sells seashells by the seashore.

(STS, SPS, SKS)
She will suggest some more tasks
Shelly grasps the risk of asking for the disks.

(L IN FRONT OF FRONT VOWELS)
I felt a chill in the newly built hotel
I still feel ill will from Bill
Phil revealed his guilt

(TR, DR, STR)
I will try to draft an attractive construction contract
He has extraordinary strength and is extremely industrious

(KT)
She asked me to connect her to neglected districts
He worked hard and liked to reflect on his mistakes

(NG)

The angry gangster strangled him with a hanger.

She keeps insisting on speaking english all morning
long.

(BEGINNING S)

Steve straightened out the style of his speech.

He stares at his screen and studies statistics.

(T FOLLOWED BY L AND N)

He'd written a title settlement for the gentlemen

I'd forgotten the metal buttons rattled.

Of course, you can also practice with traditional tongue twisters,
for instance:

If peter piper picked a peck of pickled peppers, how
many pickled peppers did peter piper pick?

THE CORK EXERCISE

Here's an additional exercise I highly recommend if you know that
you have problems with enunciation and articulation. It's going to
sound odd and you will most likely feel very silly doing it, but be
thankful that you're doing it in the privacy of your home and not
in a class – as I did, and as my students now do. You may recognize

versions of this exercise if you've seen either *The King's Speech* or *The Great Debaters*.

You will need a wine cork and a napkin or paper towel.

Place the wine cork lengthwise between your top and bottom teeth. If you have a small mouth you can cut the cork a bit. But you want to have the feeling of your mouth being stretched to its capacity. Your lips, with a lot of work, should be able to close over the cork. Keep the tip of your tongue pressed against the bottom of the cork. Do not move it. Now choose something to read. It could be a draft of a speech you're working on or it could be the morning newspaper. Read it WITH THE CORK IN YOUR MOUTH, keeping the tongue pressed against the bottom of your cork. Yes, it is going to sound ridiculous and virtually impossible to understand. It's supposed to.

After reading several sentences, remove the cork. (By now you may have figured out that the paper towel is for wiping away the excess saliva that gets produced by doing this exercise.) Now, read the same passage again. You should be able to notice how easily your tongue moves from sound to sound. You may also notice that your throat has relaxed, giving you a warmer, richer tone. Tape yourself doing this exercise and see if you can hear the difference.

## Your Sound Is Music – Stress, Pitch, and Intonation

A common problem for speakers and a complaint of listeners is that a presentation is delivered in a MONOTONE. Monotone, as the word implies, means that every word is expressed using pretty much the same pitch, volume, and tone. Speaking in a monotone doesn't give the listener clues as to what word or words you want to emphasize – what words or thoughts you think are important. It also doesn't enable the listener to feel your passion. Using a monotone will make you and your presentation seem boring and monotonous even if the material is interesting. It's a surefire way to put your audience to sleep.

To me, a speech or presentation should be compared to a great piece of music. In music there are high notes, low notes, sustained notes, staccato notes, loud horns, and soft violins. Imagine a symphony in which every note is played the same way.

Sound in movies is also extremely important. Every movie award show has several categories devoted to sound. And it's not just about being able to hear the actors' voices – the entire mood of a film can be dictated by the "score" that the director chooses to play under or through each scene. Sometimes those scores are so subtle we may not even notice them and sometimes they are so intrusive as to be distracting.

In daily speech most of us "score" our conversations naturally. When we are excited about something, our listener knows this by the way the pitch of our voice rises. When we really want to make sure someone understands what we say, we might say a word louder, linger over it longer, or pause before and after it.

However, I have found when clients start to deliver a speech or engage in a business conversation or presentation, all of that natural emphasis disappears. All I hear are words. One after another with no clue as to whether one word or word cluster has more importance than any other.

It is important when making a presentation to pay attention to emphasis, intonation, and stress. A sound designer can enhance or distract from your moviegoing experience, based on what music he chooses in a particular scene. Similarly, as a presenter, how you choose to emphasize your "focus words" or "focus thought" groups enhances or detracts from your listeners' experience.

Focus words and focus thought groups are the words or thoughts that you really want your listeners to pay attention to. They can be scored in the following ways:

- Pausing before and after
- Raising or lowering the volume
- Raising or lowering pitch
- Stressing each syllable in a word
- Slowing down or speeding up

Of course, it would be unrealistic to think that you will be able to sit down and score every presentation or conversation you have before you deliver it. Yes, Prince Albert did it in the *King's Speech,* but most of us don't have that kind of time, such a dedicated coach, or, frankly, such high stakes. There is an easier way to train your voice to be more expressive: by using the same techniques actors use.

Actors become skilled at communicating various emotions by repeatedly working on emotional scenes and monologues. You can work on adding variety and passion to your speech in the same way. On the following pages you will find several speeches from famous films. Each speech taps into strong emotions. Work on these short speeches while paying attention to the techniques I've just described: pausing, changing pitch, changing volume, changing pace, and elongating or shortening syllables. Don't be afraid to have it sound like "bad acting." You're not competing for an Oscar; you're just trying to train your "instrument." By practicing intense, almost over-the-top emphasis on strong and passionate emotion, your voice will attack your own communication in new, creative, and more expressive ways.

- Chose a paragraph from the speeches below. You can use this exercise in two ways.
- Get a recording of the original actor and practice using the exact phrasing and tonality that the actor used.
- Do NOT think about imitating the actor, but imagine circumstances under which you might use a speech like the one you chose. Then, using your own emotions and choosing the focus words you feel are important, practice the speech and decide: Where will you will pause and for how long? Which words/word groups should be louder, softer, faster, slower?
- HAVE FUN!!!

I use this exercise with all of my clients and it is extremely effective. One client came to work with me because she had just launched a new business and she was about to go to a huge conference for venture capitalists. This woman is one of the sweetest and most compassionate people I know; she is naturally soft-spoken and although extremely accomplished and intelligent can come off as self-effacing and shy. As we worked on her business pitch, I felt a definite spark was missing. When you're asking people to invest in a fledgling company, you need to have some kind of fire behind you. We worked first on punching up the word choice and on creating emotional engagement (more about that in the next section), but still her delivery lacked something. So I pulled out Michael Douglas's "Greed" Speech from the movie *Wall Street* and had her read through it. At first it was coming across just like she is: nice and compassionate. Not at all like Gordon Gekko. So I pushed her a bit (okay, maybe I pushed her a lot) and encouraged her to put herself in Gordon Gekko's shoes. He really thinks he's right and that these people who don't agree with him are complete idiots. After several attempts, she got in touch with her inner Gekko. Then, when I had her do her pitch again … WOW! It was full of fire and passion. Did she become evil or arrogant or sleazy like Michael Douglass was in the movie? No, but what she did become was a stronger, more confident, more assertive her. That's what we're aiming for with this exercise.

A common misconception many people, especially women, have is that if they use a strong, powerful voice they might be perceived as mean, bitchy, or aggressive. In my experience of working to elevate people's vocal quality, that rarely is the case. If you are intrinsically a compassionate, well-intentioned, trustworthy individual, and if your other nonverbal skills communicate those qualities, a strong, powerful voice will only make you seem more confident, assertive, and competent.

## SPEECHES

### *Mutiny on the Bounty:* Franchot Tone

These men don't ask for comfort. They don't ask for safety … They ask only (for) the freedom that England expects for every man. If one man among you believed that – one man! – he could command the fleets of England. He could sweep the seas for

England if he called his men to their duty, not by flaying their backs but by lifting their hearts.

### *Mr. Deeds Goes to Town:* **Gary Cooper**

From what I can see, no matter what system of government we have, there will always be leaders and always be followers. It's like the road out in front of my house. It's on a steep hill. Every day I watch the cars climbing up. Some go lickety-split up that hill on high, some have to shift into second, and some sputter and shake and slip back to the bottom again. Same cars, same gasoline, yet some make it and some don't. And I say the fellas who can make the hill on high should stop once in a while and help those who can't. That's all I'm trying to do with this money. Help the fellas who can't make the hill on high.

### *The Life of Emile Zola:* **Paul Muni**

Not only is an innocent man crying out for justice, but more – much more – a great nation is in desperate danger of forfeiting her honor. Do not take upon yourselves a fault, the burden of which you will forever bear in history. A judicial blunder has been committed! The condemnation of an innocent man induced the acquittal of a guilty man. And now, today, you're asked to condemn me because I rebelled on seeing our country embarked on this terrible course. At this solemn moment in the presence of this tribunal, which is the representative of human justice, before you gentlemen of the jury, before France, before the whole world, I swear that Dreyfus is innocent. By my 40 years of work, by all that I have won, by all that I have written to spread the spirit of France, I swear that Dreyfus is innocent. May all that melt away. May my name perish if Dreyfus be not innocent. He is innocent.

### *Stage Door:* Katharine Hepburn

I've learned something about love that I never knew before. You speak of love when it's too late. Help should come to people when they need it. Why are we always so helpful to each other when it's no longer any use? ... This is my home. This is where I belong. Love was in this house once, and for me it will always be here, nowhere else ... One should always listen closely when people say goodbye because sometimes they're, they're really saying farewell.

### *Mr. Smith Goes to Washington:* James Stewart

Great principles don't get lost once they come to light. They're right here. You just have to see them again ... You think I'm licked. You all think I'm licked. Well, I'm not licked. And I'm going to stay right here and fight for this lost cause, even if this room gets filled with lies like these; and the Taylors and all their armies come marching into this place. Somebody will listen to me.

*Network:* **Peter Finch**

I want you to get MAD! I don't want you to protest. I don't want you to riot – I don't want you to write to your congressman because I wouldn't know what to tell you to write. I don't know what to do about the depression and the inflation and the Russians and the crime in the street. All I know is that first you've got to get mad. (shouting) You've got to say: "I'm a human being, god-dammit! My life has value!" So I want you to get up now. I want all of you to get up out of your chairs. I want you to get up right now and go to the window. Open it, and stick your head out, and yell: "I'm mad as hell and I'm not going to take this any more! ... "

*Network:* **Faye Dunaway**

... the American people want somebody to articulate their rage for them. I've been telling you people since I took this job six months ago that I want angry shows. I don't want conventional programming on this network. I want counter-culture. I want anti-establishment. Now, I don't want to play butch boss with you people. But when I took over this department, it had the worst programming record in television history. This network hasn't one show in the top twenty. This network is an industry joke. We better start putting together one winner for next September. I want a show developed, based on the activities of a terrorist group.

### *Million Dollar Baby:* Hilary Swank

I'm 32, Mr. Dunn, and I'm here celebrating the fact that I spent another year scraping dishes and waitressing which is what I've been doing since 13, and according to you, I'll be 37 before I can even throw a decent punch, which I have to admit, after working on this speed bag for a month may be the God's simple truth. Other truth is, my brother's in prison, my sister cheats on welfare by pretending one of her babies is still alive, my daddy's dead, and my momma weighs 312 pounds. If I was thinking straight, I'd go back home, find a used trailer, buy a deep fryer and some Oreos. Problem is, this is the only thing I ever felt good doing. If I'm too old for this, then I got nothing. That enough truth to suit you?

### *Mrs. Miniver:* Henry Wilcoxon

... Why in all conscience should these be the ones to suffer? Children, old people, a young girl at the height of her loveliness. Why these? Are these our soldiers? Are these our fighters? Why should they be sacrificed? I shall tell you why. Because this is not only a war of soldiers in uniform. It is a war of the people, of all the people, and it must be fought not only on the battlefield, but in the cities and in the villages, in the factories and on the farms, in the home, and in the heart of every man, woman, and child who loves freedom! Well, we have buried our dead, but we shall not forget them. Instead they will inspire us with an unbreakable determination to free ourselves and those who come after us from the tyranny and terror that threaten to strike us down. This is the people's war! It is our war! We are the fighters! Fight it then! Fight it with all that is in us, and may God defend the right!

### *Adam's Rib:* Katherine Hepburn

... and so the question here is equality before the law – regardless of religion, color, wealth, or as in this instance, sex ... Law, like man, is composed of two parts. Just as man is body and soul, so is the law letter and spirit. The law says, 'Thou shalt not kill.' Yet men have killed and proved a reason and been set free. Self-defense – defense of others, of wife, of children and home. If a thief breaks into your house and you shoot him, the law will not deal harshly with you. Nor, indeed, should it. So here you are asked to judge not whether or not these acts were committed, but to what extent they were justified.

An unwritten law stands back of a man who fights to defend his home. Apply this same law to this maltreated wife and neglected woman. We ask you no more – Equality! ... Consider this unfortunate woman's act as though you yourselves had each committed it. Every living being is capable of attack if sufficiently provoked. Assault lies dormant within us all. It requires only circumstance to set it in violent motion. I ask you for a verdict of not guilty. There was no murder attempt here – only a pathetic attempt to save a home.

### *Network:* Peter Finch

You people and sixty-two million other Americans are listening to me right now. Because less than three percent of you people read books. Because less than fifteen percent of you read newspapers. Because the only truth you know is what you get over this tube. Right now, there is a whole, an entire generation that never knew anything that didn't come out of this tube. This tube is the gospel, the ultimate revelation. This tube can make or break Presidents, Popes, Prime Ministers. This tube is the most awesome, god – damned force in the whole godless world ...

We deal in illusions, man. None of it is true! But you people sit there day after day, night after night, all ages, colors, and creeds – we're all you know. You're beginning to believe the illusions we're spinning here. You're beginning to think that the tube is reality and that your own lives are unreal. You do whatever the tube tells you. You dress like the tube, you eat like the tube, you raise your children like the tube. You even think like the tube. This is mass madness. You maniacs. In God's name, you people are the real thing. We are the illusion. So turn off your television sets. Turn them off now. Turn them off right now. Turn them off and leave them off. Turn them off right in the middle of this sentence I am speaking to you now. Turn them off!"

## *Network*: **Beatrice Straight**

Get out, go anywhere you want, go to a hotel, go live with her, and don't come back! Because, after 25 years of building a home and raising a family and all the senseless pain that we have inflicted on each other, I'm damned if I'm going to stand here and have you tell me you're in love with somebody else! Because this isn't a convention weekend with your secretary, is it? Or – or some broad that you picked up after three belts of booze. This is your great winter romance, isn't it? Your last roar of passion before you settle into your emeritus years. Is that what's left for me? Is that my share? She gets the winter passion, and I get the dotage? What am I supposed to do? Am I supposed to sit at home knitting and purling while you slink back like some penitent drunk? I'm your wife, damn it! And, if you can't work up a winter passion for me, the least I require is respect and allegiance! (sobbing) I hurt! Don't you understand that? I hurt badly!

## *Wall Street*: **Michael Douglas**

I am not a destroyer of companies. I am a liberator of them. The point is, ladies and gentleman, that greed – for lack of a better word – is good. Greed is right. Greed works. Greed clarifies, cuts through and captures the essence of the evolutionary spirit. Greed, in all of its forms – greed for life, for money, for love, knowledge – has marked the upward surge of mankind. And Greed – you mark my words – will not only save Teldar Paper but that other malfunctioning corporation called the USA. Thank you very much."

*Lean on Me:* **Morgan Freeman**

You tried it your way for years. And your students can't even get past the Minimum Basic Skills Test. That means they can hardly read!! They've given me less than one year, one school year to turn this place around, to get those test scores up, so the State will not take us over to perform the tasks which you have failed to do! To educate our children! Forget about the way it used to be. This is not a damn democracy. We are in a state of emergency and my word is law. There's only one boss in this place, and that's me. Are there any questions?

I want all of you to take a good look at these people on the risers behind me. These people have been here up to five years and done absolutely nothing. These people are drug dealers and drug users. They have taken up space; they have disrupted the school; they have harassed your teachers; and they have intimidated you. Well, times are about to change. You will not be bothered in Joe Clark's school. These people are incorrigible. And since none of them can graduate anyway, you are all expurgated. You are dismissed! You are out of here forever! I wish you well ... My motto is simple: If you do not succeed in life, I don't want you to blame your parents. I don't want you to blame the white man! I want you to blame yourselves. The responsibility is yours!

### *A Few Good Men:* Jack Nicholson

You can't handle the truth! Son, we live in a world that has walls, and those walls have to be guarded by men with guns. Who's gonna do it? You? You, Lieutenant Weinberg? I have a greater responsibility than you can possibly fathom. You weep for Santiago, and you curse the Marines. You have that luxury. You have the luxury of not knowing what I know – that Santiago's death, while tragic, probably saved lives; and my existence, while grotesque and incomprehensible to you, saves lives. You don't want the truth because deep down in places you don't talk about at parties, you want me on that wall – you need me on that wall. We use words like "honor," "code," "loyalty." We use these words as the backbone of a life spent defending something. You use them as a punch line. I have neither the time nor the inclination to explain myself to a man who rises and sleeps under the blanket of the very freedom that I provide and then questions the manner in which I provide it. I would rather you just said "thank you" and went on your way. Otherwise, I suggest you pick up a weapon and stand the post. Either way, I don't give a damn what you think you are entitled to!

## STAYING IN CHARACTER

There's a term in acting called "breaking," which is short for "breaking character." Breaking character means that in the middle of a scene, an actor stops behaving as his character would behave. I'm sure you've seen it happen on *Saturday Night Live* and other comedy shows. The cast of *The Carol Burnett Show* used to be famous for breaking character. In the middle of a pseudo-serious scene, Harvey Korman would get the giggles and start behaving like Harvey Korman with the giggles instead of Rhett Butler talking to Scarlett O'Hara. This works okay and often adds to the humor in sketch comedies, but as you can imagine, it's the kiss of death in a serious show or in a movie. The opposite of breaking character is called "staying in character." As presenters and Star communicators, it is important to establish and stay in character from your entrance to your exit.

A friend and client of mine is a fabulous jazz singer. When she opens her mouth to sing, she is sultry, sexy, and confident. However, for years she would "break character" every time she had to deliver her introduction or between-set banter. Her Sex Symbol/Super Hero Torch Singer became an Innocent/Whiz Kid chatterbox. She over shared, was overly self-effacing, and spoke with an unconfident tone and cadence. I worked with her on her vocal tone and helped her to own the qualities and strengths that she exemplified in her singing. Then we created powerful and succinct content that she felt confident about delivering and that would be in character with the singer that her audiences came to see. The next time she performed, friends were amazed at the difference. One close friend who has known and followed her for years said that she felt like she was at a party that the singer had hosted. Oddly enough, that was *exactly* one of the images I gave the singer to imagine.

Now that you know the skills involved in making your nonverbal communication stellar, let's take a look at that all that goes into the remaining 7%: the Verbal.

# YOUR VERBAL – THE SCRIPT

According to Albert Mehrabian's study, the actual words you speak are only 7% of your message's effectiveness. But in many situations, those words make up a very important 7%. It's not ever enough to be just a pretty face. Remember, the Mehrabian statistics refer to consistency of all three elements of communication. Once your listeners decide that your presence and your vocal tone exude an impressive amount of confidence, charisma, and power, they will start to pay closer attention to your content. If your content starts to seem inconsistent with your non-verbal presentation, your listeners may start to second-guess their first impression. Once your listeners start to sense an incongruity between the way you look and sound and the actual words you are saying, they will start to feel confused, betrayed, and mistrustful. Imagine digging into an absolutely scrumptious-looking dessert that has been set in front of you, only to find out that it was made of Styrofoam. Fortunately, the process of second-guessing a first impression takes longer than the process of forming one, so let's delve into how, once you've created a positive first impression with your nonverbal communication, you can keep it with your Verbal communication.

One of the first things to know about Verbal communication is this: people usually have one question in their minds the minute you open your mouth ...

## WHAT'S IN IT FOR ME? (WIIFM)

This may sound like I'm accusing every listener of being extremely self-centered and self-serving. You may argue that many people out there genuinely want to know about other people and other people's lives. This is undoubtedly true. However, even the people who *do* want to know about you, want to know about you because something is in it for them. That something could be a personal connection or simply the enjoyment of learning someone else's story. Thinking about WIIFM does not necessarily make your listeners opportunists or mean that they don't care about you. It just means that their first instinct is to filter through your message to discover what can be gained from it.

So your 7% needs to answer your listeners' WIIFM question. But you just can't stand up and state what's in it for them. In answering the WIIFM question you need to appeal to their emotions. People take action, make decisions, and become engaged in a communication based on their emotional needs first. To engage your listeners, you need to appeal to their emotions and then present logical and practical details that support your emotional appeal. Emotional appeals come in many forms. Here is a list of some of the most common emotional appeals. This is not in order of importance. The importance depends on your topic and your listener.

## EMOTIONAL REASONS TO LISTEN

**Make your listeners feel that by listening to you they can ...**

1) make money
2) save money
3) save time
4) avoid effort
5) attain comfort
6) achieve order/cleanliness
7) improve health or attractiveness
8) escape pain
9) be more popular
10) find love
11) earn accolades/praise
12) hold onto possessions
13) be happier
14) satisfy curiosity
15) protect family
16) be in style
17) satisfy appetite
18) emulate others
19) have beautiful things

20) avoid criticism

21) take advantage of opportunities

22) be unique

23) avoid trouble

24) protect reputation

25) feel safe

26) better position socially or financially

27) be seen as powerful or influential

28) be thought intellectually superior

29) escape from reality or unpleasant situation

30) be the first to do something or to do something others can't do

31) re-experience pleasant things of the past

32) achieve or experience inner or outer peace or tranquility

You may not think about some of the above emotional appeals as being particularly emotional. However, all of these appeals tap into a basic need that a particular person might have. When people have a need that is not being met, they tend to react with their emotions.

I do not mean that to be effective communicators we must manipulate a person's emotions. That's not at all what I'm suggesting. I'm suggesting that before you can get someone to really pay attention to you, you want to give them an emotional reason to do so. Then you can share with them logical reasons to continue listening to you.

## LOGICAL REASONS TO LISTEN

**Once they feel one or more of the above emotions ... let them know ...**

- Facts that can be proven – example: *Statistics, research, experiences*
- Specific evidence or information – example: *Testimonials, case studies, reviews*
- Logical analysis of facts, reasons, and examples – example: *Your anecdotal results and experiences, demonstrations, visual support*

---

**Soap Box:**

Remember to touch your listener emotionally first because:

*"No one cares how much you know until they know how much you care."*

---

Verbal communication consists of words, phrases and sentences that touch on emotional needs; and words, phrases, and sentences that explain logical thoughts and facts. Figuring out how much of one type of verbal you need versus the other type of verbal is where the fun and creativity come in. Choosing and organizing thoughts and words into coherent presentations and exchanges is what we will work on next.

# SCRIPT WRITING 101

In 2012, the Best Picture Oscar award went to a silent film, *The Artist*. That, to me, was an amazing event. Not one that I necessarily agreed with, but notable nonetheless. In the old silent movies, the nonverbal communication skills of the actors needed to be incredibly understandable, yet nuanced and subtle. And the stories needed to be highly entertaining and/or emotionally resonant. Once "talkies" came along, however, movie themes and plots could get more complex and layered. Perhaps in the cave man era, it was enough to just communicate the WIIFT (what's in it for them). In this day and age, however, you will need to make the message you communicate more complex and layered.

Most film scripts follow a specific structure. This is referred to as the three-act structure. Film students are taught specific elements that need to be in each of the three acts and are also told on which pages specific elements should occur. The way these elements are handled by individual writers will vary greatly, and that's what makes great screenwriting. There is a strong belief and ample evidence that a screenplay carefully constructed around the three-act structure will be more successful than a screenplay that does not adhere to that structure. Since this is not a film studies book, I will not argue this point. I mention it only because a similar "Truth" exists around constructing a successful presentation and I thoroughly endorse and believe in that Truth.

Successful presentations use the following structure, which can also be broken into three acts:

I.   The Setup or Introduction – which consists of four parts
    a.   The Teaser – Attention Getter
    b.   The Hook – WIIFT (what's in it for them)
    c.   The Commercial Break – Establishing Credibility
    d.   The Preview

II.  The Plot – the Body of the presentation, which usually has three or more sections
    a)   First plot point – plus supporting details
    b)   Second plot point – plus supporting details
    c)   Third, fourth, or fifth plot points

III. The Conclusion
    a)   Recap – Review of what was just said
    b)   Closer – Resolution

Let's discuss what elements should go into each act.

## ACT I – THE SET UP/INTRODUCTION

### A) Teasers AKA Attention Getters

When I was writing for soap operas (I wrote for both *All My Children* and *One Life to Live*), each episode had to begin with a

"Teaser": a series of very short scenes that drew the audience in and made them want to stay tuned.

In films, there is usually a dramatic action sequence or a visual shown before the opening credits roll. As I mentioned earlier, this visual is called the Establishing Shot. The Teaser and Establishing Shot set the tone of the film or TV series and cue the audience as to what to expect. Similarly, an effective presentation needs to have a Teaser or attention getter to set the tone of the presentation and to cue listeners as to what they can expect. That's why it's important to start any presentation with an Attention Getter or Teaser.

**Why are Attention Getters so important?**

When you first stand in front of an audience, you cannot assume that just because you are ready to speak, they are ready to listen. A lot could be going on with them: They could have just arrived and may feel rushed and anxious about being late. They could be annoyed because they got there early and have been waiting for a while. They might be involved in a conversation with another audience member which they would like to continue. They may not particularly want to be there or they may be thinking of myriad things they need to get done. How do you get their attention? How do you convince them that it's time to stop what they are doing and listen to you?

The way most presenters begin their presentations is relatively ineffective. They usually start in one of two ways:

1) *"Good morning! My name is Joe Schmo and I'm here to talk to you about ..."*

Are you thinking, "That's the way *everybody* starts a presentation. What could be wrong with that?" What's wrong with this is that since everybody starts presentations the same boring way, listeners do not feel compelled to pay attention. First of all, your name and the topic of your presentation can be found in the program or agenda. These are things that they already know. Therefore, audience members will often continue doing exactly what they were doing until you get to what they might consider the "good part" or the meat of your presentation. Even if all eyes are on you as you dutifully give your name and the name of your presentation, your listeners' attention may be elsewhere.

The other reason not to start a presentation with your name is that, not only is it boring to your audience, it's boring to you! In the course of your lifetime, how many times have you said, "Hello, my name is ..."? How much energy and enthusiasm can you muster around that sentence? Remember how quickly listeners form an opinion about you. If the first words out of your mouth are lacking energy, enthusiasm, and passion, *and* are not audience centered, what opinion is your listener likely to make?

2) Another way some presenters start a presentation is by shouting: "*Good MORNING!!!!* Then, "*I said ... GOOD MORNING!!!"...* followed by, "*I can't hear you?*" Or, "*You can do better than that. GOOD MORNING!!!!*"

We've all seen that, right? I'm sorry, I don't know about you, but I feel that starting presentations with this type of greeting is a tad condescending. It makes me feel like before we even get to know each other, the speaker is berating me for not having enough energy or for not greeting her the "right" way. I become annoyed. I feel judged. Maybe that's just me. But why start off demanding that your audience match your energy. This might be an acceptable attention getter for a Villain, but everyone else, beware. Instead of immediately making demands on your audience, why not "tease" them into wanting to *share* their energy with you.

The way to get your listeners to pay attention and share your energy is similar to the way screen and TV writers get viewers to pay attention: we create an Attention Getter or Teaser. Here are four of the most common and most effective attention getters to use at the beginning of a presentation:

1. Ask a question or a series of rhetorical or "show of hands" questions
2. State an interesting or provocative fact or statistic
3. Tell an anecdote or short story, give an example or illustration

4. Use a well-known (not overused) or catchy quotation

There is a fifth attention getter, which I usually hesitate to give, because using it properly can be very tricky. And that is:

5. Humor – Start with a joke or a humorous observation. But make sure it's tasteful and *is* humorous!

Using one of these attention getters creates an element of surprise for your listeners. The element of surprise has the effect of causing your listeners to access a different part of their brains. Where they may have previously been focused on thoughts and behaviors in their own worlds, the element of surprise forces them to enter into the world that you are creating.

*BREAKING DOWN THE TEASERS:*

**Teaser One: Ask a question or a series of rhetorical or "show of hands" questions**

This is one of the most common attention getters because it is one of the easiest to create and is also one of the most effective. Show-of-hands questions are effective, not only because they immediately involve the audience but also because they encourage the audience to change their physical state. The act of raising the hand, and even the thought of raising the hand, activates a different area of the brain, which forces your listener to be more present. What is the difference between the two kind of questions?

**Rhetorical Questions:** These are questions you ask your audience that may or may not have an answer. Asking rhetorical questions encourages your listeners to think of answers to your questions, but does not necessarily call for them to answer the questions out loud. Example: *Are you tired of saying the same thing over and over and not being heard? Have you ever wondered why people don't listen to you? Can you think of the last time you enjoyed giving a presentation?*

**Show-of-Hands Questions:** Show of hands questions do as the name implies: they ask for a show-of-hands and usually start with the phrase, *How many of you ...* (HMOY). Example: *How many of you love giving presentations? How many of you secretly (or not so secretly) dread giving presentations? How many of you would love to feel more confident giving presentations?*

With rhetorical questions, you can often find one very thought-provoking question which will be all you need for your teaser/attention getter. *How many bits of medical data can fit onto this tiny superwidget? How long does it take to make a first impression?*

With show-of-hands questions, it is most effective to ask two or three. This allows everyone in the audience to feel as though you are acknowledging them and their feelings. If you only ask one question (for instance, "*How many of you dread giving presentations?*") and a third of the room raises their hands, two thirds of the room still does not feel acknowledged. They may dislike, but not dread, giving presentations, or they may actually love giving presentations. If you go on with the rest of your speech without acknowledging them, they may feel that you are only addressing the people who dread giving presentations and therefore your presentation is not for them. In a business environment, this is particularly important to keep in mind. People love to be acknowledged for what they already know. If you assume that your audience doesn't know something, they may feel as though you are talking down to them and may consequently feel that you have nothing to teach them. The way to avoid your audience's feeling overlooked or unacknowledged is to ask show-of-hands questions: "*How many of you have heard of the super widget? How many of you have never heard of it? How many of you are extremely familiar with how the superwidget works?*" By using those three questions you will have acknowledged pretty much all of the people in your audience. Not only that, but you will have valuable information as you as you move through the rest of your presentation. You will know how much time you will need to spend on explaining the superwidget and to what depths you may need to go.

*Important Techniques for Using Questions as an Attention Getter:*

**Show, don't tell:** You'll notice in the above show-of-hands questions, I did not preface the questions with *"Show-of-hands ..."* or say, *"Raise your hands."* The best way to encourage your audience to raise their hands is for you to do it first and show them what you expect. **Action:** As soon as you finish asking your first HMOY question, you raise your own hand. Since we, as humans, are so good at picking up visual cues, once you raise your hand, the audience will immediately understand that you are inviting them to raise theirs. This encourages people to participate physically, without coming out and telling them what to do.

Many of my clients have trouble just doing the visual cueing. They feel they need to tell the audience everything. Clients will add phrases like, *"I want to ask you a question ..."* or *"Raise your hand if ..."* This type of cushioning is not horrible, it's just not necessary. To me, it's like using training wheels on a bike when you are perfectly capable of riding without them. I stand by Nike's old slogan: "Just Do It"

**Wait for an answer!** Whenever you ask your audience a question, especially a rhetorical question, you need to pause long enough for the audience to form the answer to your question in their heads. Even though you don't expect them to answer out loud, you need to give them time to process your question and let their brains look for and formulate an answer. If you keep talking directly after you ask the question, you send a message that you didn't really care about the answer and the question was nothing more than a line in your script.

**Shorter is better:** If your questions get too long and convoluted, your audience gets lost and has no idea how to answer them. Even if the question is rhetorical, they need to be able to quickly figure out how they might want to answer it or what you would like them to focus on or think about. I have had students and clients ask questions like this: *"How would you like a piece of equipment that not only stores all of your medical data on one tiny chip, but can also be automatically traced if it gets lost?"* This is, indeed, a thought-provoking question but there are too many opportunities for listeners to get lost along the way and stop paying attention. Remember, the spoken word has to get through more barriers than the written word, and a question that looks perfectly fine on paper may sound incredibly long and complicated when it is the first thing coming out of your mouth.

### Teaser Two: State an interesting or provocative fact or statistic.

This type of teaser is very effective for persuasive types of presentations and presentations where you are explaining findings. It immediately engages your listeners by shocking them and/or educating them on the importance of your topic.

*Examples:* "Hospitals that use the superwidget have experienced a 55% drop in staff turnover." "It can take up to 12 visits to undo *a negative first impression." "Companies that engage in employee training report a 76% increase in job satisfaction."*

*"A few years ago, nearly one in five autoworkers were handed a pink slip – one in five. Four hundred thousand jobs across this industry vanished the year before I took office." President Barack Obama to the United Auto Workers, February, 28, 2012.*

If the statistic is too long or detailed, it may be helpful to have it written on a slide that you display while you read it. This is especially helpful if the statistic contains numbers and percentages. This is a great teaser for Whiz Kids and Super Heroes to use.

**Teaser Three: Tell an anecdote or short story,**

This may be the most underutilized type of teaser, but it can be very effective. People love stories. The story or anecdote can be something that has happened to you, something that has happened to somebody you knew, or even something you just heard about. As soon as you start to tell a story, the listeners begin to visualize. And by visualizing, they put themselves in your shoes or in the shoes of the person you are talking about. This creates empathy and engagement right off the bat. The important skill to learn is how to tell the story with just enough visual detail to grab interest but not so much detail that it sounds like you are rambling. I will never forget a woman in one of my trainings and her effective use of a story teaser. I had given my overview of presentation skills and talked about the four types of teasers. The participants were social service supervisors and they were to do a presentation on what they valued about the work they did. One woman started with an anecdote that went something like this: *"My office is right next door to the babies' nursery. Whenever I feel stressed or ready to give up, I walk into the nursery and look at all those tiny babies lying there ..."* I am almost 100% certain that every person in that room had an image of this woman walking around a nursery, looking at these babies. This training session took place about five years and hundreds of trainings ago, and I can still picture the woman who gave that presentation. Stories work.

**Teaser Four: A quotation**

Quotations are terrific teasers. You can quote a platitude, an advertising slogan, a politician, or any other source. As with statistics, if the quote is too long, you might want to have it in writing. Unless it's extremely recognizable, you can break my "Just do It" rule and begin by saying something like. *"One of my favorite quotes is ...,"* or, *"Ralph Waldo Emerson said ..."* This prepares your audience to listen differently. However, if you use a quote like, "To be or not to be, that is the question," You do not need to reference Shakespeare or say, *"My favorite Shakespeare quote is ..."* Famous quotes are also fun to get creative with. For example, you could open a presentation with, *"To Superwidget or not to Superwidget, that is the question."* Yes, it's a little cheesy, but depending on your audience, it could be fun.

**Teaser Five: Humor**

If you are naturally funny, you will know how to deal with this type of Teaser. If you are not naturally funny, I can't tell you what to say and I recommend not even attempting it.

*Two Rules for Using Teasers*

### 1) Tease Before You Tell

If you'll notice, most television shows now begin with their version of a teaser – a short scene – before they start rolling the credits and sometimes even before they flash the theme song or the title of the show. Why? Because something that grabs a viewer's interest is more likely to ensure that the viewer will not switch channels.

Things used to be different before there were so many options on television. Television shows used to start with just the theme song and the title of the show. Why? Because they knew that most viewers were committed to watching their favorite show no matter what the particular episode was about. Nowadays, viewers have more choices, so shows need to involve them in the story line as quickly as possible. The same is true of giving a presentation, chairing a meeting, sharing an elevator pitch, or answering interview questions. Listeners have choices. They have the physical choice to attend, not attend, or leave in the middle. They also have the mental choice to daydream, check e-mails, or play Angry Birds on their iPad. This is why it is so imperative to give them a teaser *before* you "roll your credits."

To be clear: What I am suggesting is that you stand in front of an audience and have the *very first* words coming out of your mouth be one of the four teasers outlined above. You do not even need to say, "*Good morning,*" or "*Good afternoon,*" or "*Thanks for coming.*" "*Thanks for having me*" before the teaser.

Many of my clients find this challenging. They have had it drilled into them that the way to start a presentation is to say, "*Hello, my name is ... And I'm going to talk about ...*" They argue that it seems rude not to do this first. I'm sure many television executives balked at the thought of opening a show with a scene and not with the title of the show. I'm sure they argued that it might seem intrusive to the viewer. However, I'm also sure that after a bit of market research on viewer engagement when a teaser is used versus when it is not used, they found using a teaser to be highly effective. If you don't want to take my word for it, I urge you to try your own market research. Call a small meeting of peers and colleagues or just friends. Prepare a brief presentation and start with a teaser. Gauge the listeners' reaction and, most importantly, gauge your own level of engagement. All of my clients and students admit that when they jump right into a presentation, it makes them feel more connected to the audience and to the material. Feeling that immediate connection will give you more energy and make you more engaged and engaging.

## 2) Don't Tease and not Deliver

Imagine seeing an advertisement for a fabulous Italian restaurant. The ad tells you about the delicious sauces, the authentic Italian atmosphere; it might even talk about customer satisfaction. You go to the restaurant and the waiter puts a menu in front of you that lists all Vietnamese dishes. Whether or not you like Vietnamese food, or whether or not this restaurant serves some of the best Vietnamese food on the planet, you will undoubtedly be disappointed since you were expecting an Italian feast.

Sometimes, when I tell clients to think up teasers for their presentations, they create these wonderful, dramatic, thought-provoking, or engaging teasers ... but these teasers have little or nothing to do with the core message of the presentation that is being delivered. This is a problem. Listeners will feel let down, disappointed, and confused if you engage them with a great teaser and then start talking about something that does not directly relate to what you engaged them with. Think back on our Italian restaurant analogy. The first thing you would probably do is to check to make sure you are in the right place. Then you would ask if the waiter has, by some chance, brought the wrong menu. Then you would more than likely get angry at the advertising source that steered you in the wrong direction. This is similar to your listeners' thought process as they try to find the connection to a teaser that does not match up with the content of the presentation. It's confusing and frustrating, and can be maddening.

To avoid this type of audience distraction, make sure that your teaser clearly creates engagement and causes people to think about the core message of your presentation. I will talk more about the core message in the next section.

A)  **Station Identification** – Now is the time in your presentation where you can say hello, say your name if they don't know it already or repeat it if they do, and thank or acknowledge as many people as you like. Hopefully with your engaging, provocative attention getter, you have intrigued your listeners enough that they want to know who you are. By creating an engaging teaser that connects you to your audience and your audience to your material, you have shown that you are inviting and authentic. Now when you thank them for coming or tell them how glad you are to be there, they will be more inclined to believe you.

## B) The Hook – AKA – What's in It for Them (WIIFT)

A TV show or movie could have an intriguing teaser but eventually will need to let the viewer know more about that particular episode. That's when they present you with "a Hook": an event, a question, or a problem that will take you the entire episode or movie to figure out.

No matter how engaging your teaser is, your audience will still want the answer to the classic question, "What's in this for me?" Now that you have their attention, it is time to drop them "a Hook" – let them know what they can expect to learn from listening to you.

The Hook or WIIFT section of your introduction is where you assure your listeners that your presentation will be relevant, enlightening, necessary, and, at the very least, interesting. Your WIIFT statement should also contain your core message.

**Example: (Teaser)** Did you know that it can take up to 12 visits to undo a negative first impression? (**Brief Commercial**): Good morning, my name is Robyn Hatcher and (**WIIFT**) I'm here because I am passionate about the art of communication. I promise that by the end of this presentation you will know skills and techniques to make sure that your first impression will be a lasting one.

People take action, make decisions, and become engaged or interested in something or someone for emotional reasons first and logical reasons second. The Hook should tap into your listeners' emotions. It should let them know that there will be an emotional reward for them if they continue listening. Depending on your audience and your topic, there may be several emotional reasons that resonate with your listener. In the above example the reward is that after listening to this presentation you will be able to make a killer first impression. If you look back on the list of "Emotional Appeals," being able to make a killer first impression could touch on these emotional appeals: (9) be popular, (10) attract the opposite sex, (11) gain praise, (16) be in style, (20) avoid criticism, (22) be individual, (26) better position socially or financially, (27) be seen as powerful or influential.

I could even target it more specifically if I knew the general makeup of my audience. What if I knew I was talking to job seekers?

Example: (Teaser) How many of you are excited to be job searching? How many of you are getting frustrated with your job search? Research shows that employers decide within four minutes whether or not they are going to hire you. (Brief Commercial) Good morning, my name is Robyn Hatcher. (WIIFT) I am passionate about the art of communication and today I'm going to give you skills and techniques to help make sure that the first four minutes of your next job interview will be effective and engaging and will have employers wanting to see more.

Before your next presentation, think about what emotional need might move your listeners. Refer back to the list of emotional triggers that move people to make decisions or become engaged. (on page 184) and see how you can create a WIIFT statement that touches on some of those emotional needs.

## C) Major Commercial Break – Establishing Credibility

If the audience doesn't know you, this is where you can briefly explain why you are the perfect person to speak on this topic. Sometimes even if the audience does know you, depending on your topic, you might want to share with them what qualifies you or moves you to talk about this particular topic.

Some people suggest that the speaker ask permission to share information about him/herself. *"Since we're going to be spending the next 60 minutes together, do you mind if I tell you a little about myself?"* I'm not married to that technique. Sometimes I do it, sometimes not. More often I will continue after my WIIFT statement by saying something like, "One of the reasons I'm so passionate about this topic is ... (Here I would add a piece of my personal story)." And then add. "For the past 18 years I have been helping people ... (And here I would give a brief rundown of some of my pertinent experiences.)

*TIPS FOR DELIVERING CREDIBILITY:*

**Use specific details**

- How many years have you been doing what you're doing?
- Where did you learn to do what you do?
- How many people have you helped, worked with?
- What quantifiable results have you achieved?

Numbers are good here. This is the time for any name dropping that you think might add to your credibility. If you are now thinking, "I don't want to sound like I'm bragging." This is the time to reframe what you think bragging means. It is not bragging to share important information about yourself that enables your listener to trust you and, therefore, allows the presentation you are about to share to have more relevance.

**If you don't need or don't have the experience?**

If you feel your numbers or experience are not impressive enough, or if you are presenting in front of colleagues who know all your details, this is the part of the introduction where you can talk about your story – highlighting your passion for the topic and what drove you to become the expert you are today, the research you've done on the topic, or your desire to help and inform your audience. When speaking in front of colleagues who may know everything about you, it might be effective to remind them of some of the experiences you have had that are relevant to the core message of your current presentation.

**How and when to use your personal story in your Commercial Break:**

As I mentioned earlier, people love stories. Stories sell. A personal story can create immediate rapport between you and your listeners. Personal stories are a terrific part of the Commercial Break if you're presenting to a large group of people who do not know you and if you are selling a service or a product that you created. And, of course, for motivational or inspirational presentations, your personal story is essential.

As with the archetypical themes used to create screenplays, there are archetypical themes you can use to help you decide what type of personal story you want to include in your introduction.

1.  Transformation – How you transformed yourself or a situation from a failure to a win.
2.  Redemption – How you, a small "David," won over a huge "Goliath."
3.  Miracles/Magic Bullet – Something was wrong or broken and something you did, learned, or created fixed what was wrong.
4.  Mythic or Epic – An amazing, unbelievable event or journey either physical or spiritual that happened to you.

Any of these themes can be terrific rapport-and credibility-building additions to your introduction. For example, for a new audience I usually talk about how my nickname growing up was "Shy" – a Transformation Themed story. And many people who I meet years after I've given a presentation will remember me because of my "Shy" story. Stories not only help people relate to you, they help them remember you.

However, it's important to remember to relate *why* you are telling the story. The story should have a direct relationship to the bottom line of your speech, otherwise people will feel that it is self-indulgent and a waste of their time. I relate my story to the meat of my presentation in several ways: First, if somebody as shy as I was can be up here doing what I'm doing, then no matter how much you hate public speaking, you can succeed. Second, because I was so shy, I know what it's like to change and I know what it takes to change. And third, being shy taught me so much about the art of communication, because I got to observe how other people communicated and I learned what works and what doesn't work.

I was recently at a entrepreneur conference where a woman told a story about her whole family being robbed. Her topic was Brand Identity. You might wonder what getting robbed has to do with brand identity, but she was able to relate the story by explaining that after the robbery she realized that the important thing in life was her family and that being robbed and seeing the possibility of losing her family showed her that she needed to rebrand her own life. Not an obvious connection but it worked. If your story is interesting enough, it's often possible to find a way to make it connect to your topic. I've had amazing success, teasing out a client's story and then finding a way to relate it to their mission or bottom line.

**Soap Box**

Be *very* vigilant about editing your story so that it is short and concise. Your Setup should not be more than seven minutes. People do not need to know what color the carpet was in the room or the specific names of each character. They don't need to know specific dialogue. Think about this piece of your personal story as an overview of the whole story and include only the details that will create enough visual information for your audience to be able to see you in the situation and then be able to see the change you describe. It's often possible to refer back to your story at another point in your presentation and add more details. And if your audience would like more details, they will ask you at the end of your presentation, which will create another opportunity to expand your relationship and rapport.

### D) Preview – State your purpose

The Preview is where you tell your the listeners more specifically what they will be getting from the presentation. If you are doing a formal presentation using slides and visuals, this is where you would present the agenda, the objectives, or the overview. The Preview differs from The Hook or WIIFT in that where the WIIFT statement gives the emotional benefits your listeners will gain, the Preview includes more practical and logical benefits. If your presentation were a vacation, The Hook or WIIFT would be the travel brochure and the Preview would be the itinerary. The

Preview is where you can finally say the sentence that you are dying to utter: "Today I'm going to talk about ...," although there are still more interesting ways to say it.

**Examples:**

*"Today I'm going to share with you techniques to improve your nonverbal communication, skills to help you identify your specific communication style, and tips on how to create an engaging elevator pitch."*

*"By the end of this presentation you will know three ways to improve the performance of your Superwidget." (briefly list the three ways)*

*"Over the next 60 minutes we'll be discussing five ways you can improve your credit score." – (briefly list the five ways.)*

The **Teaser**, the **Station Identification**, the **Hook**, the **Commercial Break**, and the **Preview** make up the five essential parts of the introduction or speech "Setup." Aside from the Teaser coming before everything else, the order of the other four parts is not etched in stone. They can be interchanged to some extent, although it's better to have the Preview come last so that you can smoothly transition from the Preview to the first of the main points you've outlined. Even though the introduction has four specific parts, an introduction does not need to be more than three to seven minutes. If you make your intro much longer than five minutes, (seven if your story is an engaging one), your listeners will grow impatient while waiting for the meat.

I spend a good deal of my coaching time helping my clients create solid introductions. I suggest you do the same. Once you have a solid and engaging introduction, the rest of the presentation will flow a lot more easily. This does not mean the introduction needs to be the first part of the presentation you create, however. Sometimes it's helpful to create an outline for your speech first and that outline will inform you of what your Teaser, WIIFM, and Preview should be.

After the introduction is delivered, it's time to get to the "Plot" or the "Body" of your presentation.

## ACT II – THE "PLOT" OR THE "BODY":

In the Setup of a film we are introduced to the characters and the plot themes. Then, in the subsequent acts, the screenwriter expands more on the actual plot. You find out more about the characters and what the writer wants us to learn, feel, or take away from the story.

In a presentation script, the part that expands on, and gives details about, the main ideas you've introduced in your Setup is called the "Body." The body is broken up into several sections. Each section should be giving information and supporting one of the main ideas that you identified in your Preview (the part where you've told your listeners exactly what you are going to cover.) The first part of your presentation will go into detail about the first point or main idea you spoke about; the second part will detail your second point, and so on.

If your Preview went like this: *"Today I'm going to go over the three steps we'll need to take before implementation can happen: First, we need to have all the legal documents filed; second, we need to agree on our timeline; and third, we need to create our working schedule."*

You would then transition from the Preview by saying something like, "Let's start with the legal forms that need to be filed." And you would proceed to let the people in the room know how, what, when, where, and why the legal forms need to be filed.

Good filmmakers do not simply have the characters of their film come out and tell you what's going on or what they want you to feel. Good filmmakers show you what is going on and what the characters want and feel by using techniques that get you to feel, experience, and empathize along with their characters.

During the body of a presentation, good speakers also need to use techniques to get their listeners to feel, experience, and empathize with their main points. Based on the preview example above, the speaker could say, *"Let's start with the legal forms that need to be filed ..."* and then say, *"I need you to make sure all the documents are filed by June 15 or else the project has no chance of being completed on schedule."* However, a communication like that could come off as brusque and aggressive. A direct approach like this might be an appropriate way to present the information if the project had been dragging on for a long time or had been previously discussed.

But imagine, as was the case with one of my clients, that this was new information and it needed to be shared with representatives from a large important corporation and that my client, the person leading the meeting, needed to present himself to these representatives as a competent, trustworthy partner who would be in charge of pulling off a very large and costly project for this large important corporation. A brusque, assertive communication could set up an antagonistic relationship that would not be beneficial for the future of the project. So let's explore ways that my client could communicate the same information in a more engaging way.

Once a main idea is presented, a good speaker should weave both emotional and logical details that support the main idea and engage the listeners. Some effective ways to support the main ideas of a presentation are:

- **Specific examples** – give a specific example from your own personal experience (or from a related experience) of how an idea, concept, or technique you are presenting may have worked in the past. *"Example has far more followers than reason." – Christian Boyle*
- **Stories** – similar to examples, but stories can be more allegorical and may be only thematically connected to your topic.

- **Visual language** – use descriptive language that creates pictures in your listener's mind.

- **Definitions** – dictionary definitions are great ways to expand on the meaning of certain well-known words or concepts.

- **Quotes** – in the body of the presentation, quotes don't need to be well known but should be from reputable sources or people related to the topic. If quotes are long, having them in writing is most helpful.

- **Statistics** – always helpful but should be dramatic enough to have an impact, yet not so complicated that they lead to confusion. Some professionals are mistrustful of statistical information, so statistics should not be the *only* type of logical support you use.

- **Comparisons/analogies** – comparing something you are trying to explain with something that is already very familiar to your audience is a very effective way to get people to understand and remember your point. (In case you haven't realized it by now, this whole book is written as an analogy and hopefully, it's been effective.)

- **Visual aids** – It can be helpful to have an actual object or photo to show to your listeners in addition to any slide show software you may choose to use.

- **Repetition** – Don't be afraid to repeat important points. If you say something in the introduction of your presentation, you can and often should repeat it in the first, second, and or third acts. People forget 40% of a presentation in one hour, 60% in a day and 90% in a week. So repetition is important. And if you're worried that people will think you're having a senior moment, you can always reference your repetition by saying something like, *"As I've already mentioned ..."* OR *"I'd like to reiterate ..."*

Using one or two of the above techniques, how might you create your first plot point and explain the need for that June 15 filing deadline? Here's the preview again: *Today I'm going to go over the three steps we'll need to take before implementation can happen; First, we need to have all the legal document filed, second, we need to agree on our timeline, and third, we need to create our working schedule."*

**Possible answer:** "First, let's talk about filing the necessary documents. I know how important the October 20th launch date is for you. The sooner this project is implemented and running, the more efficient the division will be. In order to ensure we meet that deadline, there are five legal waivers that need to be filed by June 15th. Getting these documents filed is like laying the foundation for a building. It is what will enable us to get started on and build out the project. Here (showing visual) is a list of the five documents we need; this is a breakdown of who needs to file which document and what information needs to be obtained. We recently completed a similar project for a company that was just about your size and because that company filed the necessary documents early, we were actually able to complete the project a week ahead of schedule. We'd love to be able to do that for you."

Can you identify which techniques I used? For extra credit, create a Preview for a presentation you need to deliver or have delivered in the past. Now take the information from that preview and create your first plot point.

_____

_____

_____

_____

## IMPROVING YOUR SECOND ACT

**How to keep your audience engaged!**

For screenwriters, the hardest part of a script is the second act. Once you have created a great setup, laid out the theme of the movie, and created a suspenseful Hook, or in our case a WIIFT, you now have a substantial amount of time to keep the audience's interest before you get to the payoff and the conclusion. Entire books are written about how to write an effective second act. To energize the second act, most film writers start adding plot twists. Every time you take the plot in a direction that the audience does not expect, you have engaged the audience a bit more, which will, hopefully, sustain their interest.

In delivering a speech or presentation, you don't necessarily want to create twists in your plot, but you do want to keep the audience engaged and interested. The techniques above – examples, stories, analogies, etc. – will help, but sometimes audiences may need an extra pick-me-up. If you are giving a rather long presentation, or if you feel the audience's energy lag, try out some of the following tips:

- **Ask questions** – If you start to see that the energy in a particular audience is dragging, ask a targeted open-ended question and ask the audience to either call out an answer or raise their hands to answer. (See the section on Questions & Answers to ensure this doesn't derail your presentation.)

- **Ask for volunteers** – Have an activity ready that you would like to demonstrate or role-play and ask someone from the audience to come up and be in the hot seat. If you get no volunteers, use the "Army method" and call on someone; few people will refuse and, if they do, don't take it personally and ask someone else. (This is where being able to pick up on body language cues will be really useful. Look for someone who is in an open position, has been giving you eye contact, and has been nodding occasionally at what you're saying.)

- **Use humor** – Of course, as always with humor, it needs to be appropriate to your audience. As a presenter, if you are going to use humor, you also have to be prepared in the event people do not laugh. Self-deprecating humor will generally work for most types – especially Comics, Whiz Kids, Curmudgeons, and Innocents. However, it is very important to know when self-deprecating humor becomes over-sharing. That makes the audience feel uncomfortable; instead of laughing with you, they are embarrassed.

- **Ask for a show of hands** – Create another "How many of you" (HMOY) question and indicate (by raising your hand) that you want them to raise their hands. This will perk up your listeners mentally by getting them to think of an answer to your question and physically by encouraging them to change their physical state by raising their hands.

- **Encourage State Changes** – Speaking of changing physical states: for a longer presentation, you can ask people to stand and stretch; give the person next to them a high-five or a shoulder massage; or repeat something you just said to the person next to them. This technique of allowing your listeners to make a physical change will bring a different energy to your presentation and help your audience to feel more present.

- **Create Partner or Group Shares** – This is the ultimate state change. Partner or Group shares can be used for a longer presentation and/or for a presentation where there may be an activity that you would like the participants to experience. However, this technique can also work for a simple informative presentation. You can give the audience a question or a situation to discuss with a partner; or after delivering a section of your material, you can ask your listeners to share with their partners their thoughts about what you just delivered. **Example:** If I had just taught the above section on Audience Engagement, I might ask for a partner or group share and set it up with these questions: "*As a presenter, have you ever used any of the above audience engagement techniques? Have you ever been in an audience where one of these techniques was used? Discuss your experience. Was the particular technique helpful? Why or why not?* (**Always be prepared for rascals:** If someone says neither of these things is in their realm of experience, then ask them to think about which technique they think might be helpful and why.)

It's important when using partner exercises to be very clear and organized with your instructions. I've learned this the hard way. Audience members are easily confused by verbal instructions and if you rely solely on verbal instructions you will need to repeat them clearly several times. A good trick is to ask one of the audience members to repeat what they heard the instructions to be. Because I've experienced so much confusion around giving verbal instruction, now when I do partner exercises, I make a point of writing the instructions out on a slide and or in the handouts that I create.

In order to successfully deal with partner exercises, it is important to:

- Organize how and when the people break into partners
- Be clear about what you expect them to talk about (writing it down is helpful)
- Give clear instruction as to how much time you are going to give them (time per person or total time)
- Let them know whether you will tell them when to switch

After the agreed-upon time has passed, ask if anyone would like to share something about what was discussed. If no one volunteers, wait a few moments and then use your Army method of volunteering and call on someone.

## CONNECTING THE DOTS – TRANSITIONS

Film editing is one of the most important jobs in the movie industry, yet few people outside of the industry appreciate what an editor does. The film director shoots hours upon hours of film and it's the editor's job to put all the footage together in a way that makes the movie look seamless. Good editing usually goes unnoticed to the average viewer but bad editing is obvious; bad editing results in jumpy, disjointed cuts that can be confusing for the viewers and will affect the overall believability of the film. What makes good editing good is the use of transitions.

Transitions are also what good speakers use to help their presentations feel seamless, understandable, and easy to follow. Transitions are used to join or edit together the different sections of a presentation. You should use transitions to move from the introduction to the body of your presentation and from one main point of the body to another main point and from the body to the conclusion.

Film editors use several different types of transitions or editing techniques, some more obvious than others. There are films that use text on the screen to tell the viewer how much time has gone by or what city or country the film is now in. Some films find a connection between an image in one scene and the image of the next scene for a more subtle transition. And, of course, some films just "jump cut" (an abrupt movement of a subject on the screen) with no smooth transition. In speeches, there are obvious transitions and more subtle transitions as well. Jump cutting in a speech is not advised.

Obvious transitions remind the listeners of what was just said and prepares them for what's to come. Obvious transitions are very effective for technical, instructional, or informative presentations. Subtle transitions are more suited to inspirational or motivational speeches.

You need transitions because you want your listeners to know where you are taking them and what you are planning to share with them. Without transitions, especially in data-heavy presentations, your listeners may get distracted and confused and they may start to feel anxious and frustrated.

I often explain the need for transitions by comparing a speech to a train ride. Your attention getter and introduction entice your audience or train passengers to take a trip with you. Once they are on your train, however, you can't just speed off without making sure that your passengers are comfortable and committed to continuing on with the journey. Imagine that you are in Philadelphia and you get on a train to Boston. Now imagine that the train speeds off and stops occasionally, but never announces the name of the stop. You might feel confident that you would eventually get to Boston since upon boarding you were told the train was heading to Boston. You might even think that you will know when you get to Boston because you know how long the trip is supposed to take. But I would bet that if the train continued to speed along without reassuring you that you are heading in the right direction, you might begin to feel a little nervous. A similar effect happens to listeners of a presentation. They know that you will not talk forever and they hope that they will learn something from you along the way, but without transitions they begin to feel anxious. By using transitions, you eliminate that anxiety.

**Examples of obvious transitions:** *"Now that we have established X ... let's take a look at Y and Z ..." "In addition to doing A, B, and C ... it's important to also learn how to D ..." "I hope it's clear what X does ... now let me explain ..." "You now know ... Let's move on to ..."*

**More subtle transitions:** *"As you can see ..." "Another technique/ piece of advice I'd like to share with you is ..." "That's not the only thing I learned ..." "If that's not bad enough ..." "If you only remember one thing I say today, I'd like you to remember ..."*

The type of transition you use will depend on the material you are delivering and your delivery style. Whiz Kids, Super Heroes, and Curmudgeons will feel more comfortable with the obvious transition, whereas other types may be more suited to using subtle ways to connect their material.

## ACT III – ALL'S WELL THAT ENDS WELL – CONCLUSION/RESOLUTION

The outline for all speeches can be summed up by this adage: *"Tell them what you're going to tell them. Tell them. Then tell them what you told them."* The conclusion of your presentation is where you tell them what you've told them.

Once you've presented all of your main points, it's time to bring your presentation to a close. But after having taken your listeners on a great journey, you don't want to abruptly dump them at their destination. You want to deliver them to their destination gently and maybe with some souvenirs from their trip. It can be frustrating to be thoroughly involved and engaged in a movie and then suddenly it's over and nothing is resolved.

The best way to conclude a presentation is to create a resolution or conclusion in which you:

- Briefly repeat and summarize the main ideas you presented.
- Remind the audience of your What's In It for Them and remind them of how they are now better informed, prepared, enlightened because of your presentation.
- Then give them a memorable souvenir, or a "Closer." It's important for the final impression of you to be as memorable as the first impression.

*EFFECTIVE CLOSERS:*

**Reference or re-word the Teaser that you used at the beginning of your speech.**

For example, if the attention getter/Teaser was: *"How many of you love to speak in public? How many of you would rather go to the dentist? How many of you would like to feel more confident speaking in public?"* You might close with something like, "After today's presentation, if you ever have to choose between going to the dentist and speaking in public, I hope I've given you enough skills and techniques to confidently choose to speak in public."

**Or you can create a new, more powerful Closer related to your bottom line.**

If the bottom line for your presentation was to give your listeners the confidence to speak in public, your closer could be: *"For those of you who were afraid of speaking in public, let me leave you with this quote: 'Courage is fear that has said its prayers'. I'm hoping the techniques I shared with you today were the prayers you needed to give you the courage to tackle your next speaking opportunity with the utmost confidence."*

Notice how both closers end by expressing hope or desire about the future. For informative and inspirational presentations, adding positive reinforcement will help the listeners remember and feel positive about you and your presentation.

### CALL-TO-ACTION CLOSERS

For more persuasive presentations – political speeches, sales presentations, pitches – it's important for the last part of the Closer be a call to action. I sometimes coach teams and individuals who need to pitch a new idea or a project to venture capitalists, businesses, or other organizations. It's amazing how many times they fail to come out and ask for what they want.

Note: For pitches, it's important to mention your call to action in the beginning of the presentation also (it would be placed near the WIIFT) and then again at the end.

**Example:**

WIIFT "... that's why, today, we are asking you to invest $500,000 towards the creation of the mobile skin cancer detection center ... ."

**Closer/Call to Action:** After hearing about the benefits, the profitability, and the need for our mobile center, we strongly hope you will consider an investment of $500,000 towards its creation. **Remember:** the conclusion is just as, if not more, important than the opening. Don't throw it away.

In the section above, I've given you a basic outline for creating and organizing almost any type of presentation. But an outline needs to be fleshed out; you need to gather material that will turn your outline into an engaging piece of communication. If you struggle to achieve this, here is some help.

## YOUR BOTTOM LINE – THE THEME

In film-writing classes, instructors discuss the importance of having an overall theme for the film and how some themes are more universally accepted than others. Popular themes for successful movies are Redemption, Salvation, Transformation, and Boy Meets Girl. In speech writing, instead of themes, people talk about your bottom line or your core message.

Your core message, bottom line, or theme can be described as your reason for verbalizing any speech, presentation, or conversation.

To discover your bottom line, ask yourself this question: If there is only one thing I want my listeners to remember, it's ...? The answer to that question should be your bottom line. The bottom line should be stated in the WIIFT and, like the theme of a movie, should be woven throughout each main idea or plot point of the presentation and then repeated again in the conclusion.

---

**Try it:**

The one thing I want my listener to remember is:

_____

_____

_____

---

Once you've figured out your bottom line; ask yourself these questions:

- Who is my listener/audience?
- How much time do they have?
- What do my listeners already know?
- What more do they need to know?
- What will engage my listeners' emotions?
- What will appeal to my listeners' logic?

A great visual tool to help you brainstorm and discover what information should go into the body of the presentation or conversation is the Mind Map.

## MIND-MAPPING

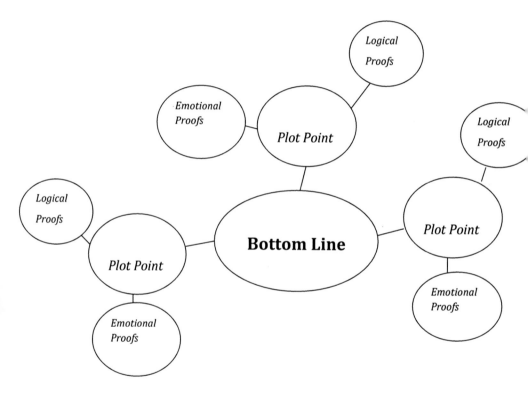

Now think of a presentation or conversation you would like to prepare for and create a mind map for it.

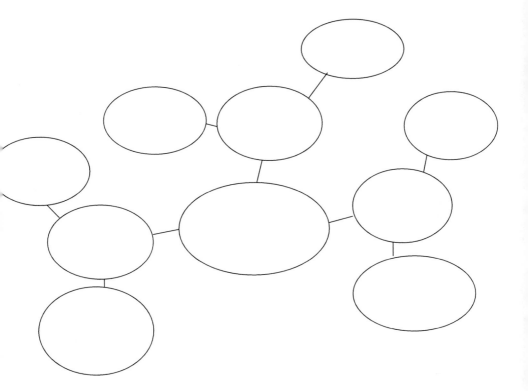

I've shared with you all of the behind-the-scenes secrets to creating and delivering an ovation-winning presentation. You know your ActorType and how to make it work for you. You know how to make your nonverbal communication powerful and you know how to create and organize a relevant presentation. Now it's time to add the "it factor"!

# VALUE – THE "IT" FACTOR

There has been much talk in recent years about Personal Branding. Entrepreneurs and small businesses are encouraged to brand themselves. Individual business professionals are also being encouraged to develop their personal brand and express it within their company or organization. I agree in principle with the concept of personal branding; however, I'm not crazy about the way this process can be interpreted. When most people think of the word "brand," they envision huge corporations with recognizable logos. Or they think of the Old West when livestock was "branded" with a fiery hot iron. Nothing in either of those images seems to be "personal." Instead of "personal brand," I prefer to use the term "Value Proposition," or in keeping with the theme of this book, The "It" Factor. The semantic difference for me is that a brand seems to imply something which you have to discover and then display externally. Whereas Value and "It" imply something that you already own. I don't believe you have to *discover* your "It" Factor as much as you have to *uncover* it.

In the 1920s actress Clara Bow was declared the "It" Girl because of her charm, wit, sex appeal, vitality, and professionalism – and because she embodied the newly liberated woman. Even though most of her performances were in silent films, people could tell she had "It" and were enthralled by her.

Many people feel that you are either born with "It" or you're not. Undoubtedly, charm and charisma come more easily to some people than to others. However, I truly believe that we all have a tremendous ability to become charismatic individuals.

## Uncovering Your "It" Factor

A very interesting article about charisma was published in the *Scientific American Mind* (Haslam and Reicher, "In Search of Charisma," *Scientific American Mind*, July/August 2012). The article cites research done on charisma and leadership and concludes that whereas most of us believe that leaders possess charisma and therefore enthrall followers, research points to the fact that followers "confer" charisma onto their leaders based on the followers' perception of how much the leader is like them and how much success the leader has achieved. "As (sociologist Max) Weber (states): What is alone important is how the individual is regarded by those subjected to charismatic authority, by his 'followers' or 'disciples,' in other words, followers distinguish the leader from others and *confer* charisma on him or her." (Haslam and Reicher, "In Search of Charisma," *Scientific American Mind*, July/August 2012). Clara Bow had the "It" factor because she exhibited qualities that Americans at that time wanted to embody and extol.

The *Scientific American Mind* article uses Franklin Roosevelt as an example of charisma or having had the "It" factor. As an invalid he did not possess the "normal" attributes of a virile, robust leader.

So what did he do? The article asserts: "Numerous scholars suggest that he derived it [charisma] by artfully turning his disadvantage into an advantage. He shifted the focus from the negative qualities of his condition to *the positive attributes of his personal conquest* – courage, endurance and effort. Doing so allowed him to connect personally with the suffering of millions of ordinary Americans during the Great Depression."(Emphasis mine)

So, how do you uncover your "It" Factor? How do you ensure that people "confer" charisma on you?

- **Focus on your positive attributes:**

  It seems simple and obvious to say focus on the positive. But how many of us really do that? In the beginning of this book where I listed the positive attributes associated with your ActorType, how many of those attributes did you fully identify with? Now compare that to how many qualities listed under Fatal Flaws you owned up to.

  Your positive attributes are what make up your "It" Factor – just as FDR's made up his and led to his overwhelming popularity.

  **Try this:**
  o   Write down all the positive attributes you possess. (If you did the exercise around choosing your wardrobe, you already have a list to work from.) Even if you feel

a seed of an attribute that is underdeveloped, write it down.

o   Write down detailed examples of how you have used each attribute in a given situation. It does not have to be work related. It does not even have to have been recent. If you get stuck, ask a close friend or colleague to help you.

o   For attributes you don't fully embody yet, "Own it while you hone it" or "Act till it's a fact." These are phrases I coined to counteract the popular expression, "*Fake it till you make it.*" Let's be honest, nobody likes a fake and few people feel comfortable feeling like they are faking something. If a particular positive attribute is not fully integrated into your behavior, write down examples of how you would like to use that quality. Write it in positive, present-tense sentences just as you wrote for qualities that you are actually using. Then act as though that desired quality were fully realized. Adopt the body language, vocal tone, word choice, and, most importantly, the mind set of someone with that attribute.

One of the saddest experiences I've ever had as a coach was when I talked to a woman who was an incredibly hard worker and invaluable to the day- to-day workings of her company. I asked her to tell me what value she brought to this business. She looked at me in all seriousness, and said she couldn't tell me. I showed her a list of positive adjectives and asked her to use that list to tell me what positive qualities she possessed. She still couldn't do it. It is little wonder that she felt overwhelmed and underappreciated. How can someone appreciate you when you are not clear on what you deserve to be appreciated for?

- **Connect:**

According to Haslam and Riecher, a reporter asked an upset mourner at FDR's funeral whether he had known the president. The mourner replied, "No, but he knew me." Having that type of connection with your staff, your colleagues, or the audience at your presentation will instantly add to your "It" factor.

Throughout this book I have spoken about how important it is to connect with your listener. I've shared connecting techniques like:

- o Focusing on what you have to give and not what people think of you.
- o Organizing your content around What's in it For Them.
- o Using teasers to get your audience's attention before you begin your presentations.
- o Telling your personal story.
- o Asking questions to make sure you understand a person's needs.

Other techniques important for connecting:

- o Listening.

o   Using language that is inclusive – "us" and "we" vs. "I" and "you."

To quote "In Search of Charisma" again: "A charismatic leader is an entrepreneur of identity. This person clarifies what we believe **rather than telling people what they believe.**" (Emphasis theirs)

- **Share what you care about:**

    Expressing your positive attributes and connecting with listeners is not always enough to give you that "It" factor. Most charismatic people have strong values and beliefs that they embody and make a point of infusing those values and beliefs into their communication and presentation style.

    In recent years, there has been a plethora of top celebrities, each coming out in support of a particular cause or charity. Some have initiated their own causes and charities. In doing this, the celebrity is sharing what they care about. The values and beliefs of the charity or cause usually align with a specific value that the celebrity wants to embody; the embodiment of that value adds to their "It" Factor. Few people can think of Angelina Jolie without thinking of her commitment to children and Africa. Bono seems to be known now more for his activism than for his music. In sharing with the world what they value in life, these celebrities have gone from being talented entertainers to being charismatic leaders.

You do not have to go out and donate or raise millions of dollars for a cause. However, what you can do is learn to weave your values into your communication.

**Try This:**

o   If you took the VIA Character survey that I mentioned in Chapter One, you can refer back to your first five character strengths.

o   You can also look at the list of values below and self-select five values that you feel strongly about. Values that you feel you exemplify on a daily basis, or that you want to exemplify.

# WHAT DO YOU VALUE?

| | | |
|---|---|---|
| Achievement | Friendships | Physical challenge |
| Accuracy | | |
| Advancement and promotion | Growth | Pleasure |
| Adventure | Having a family | Power and authority |
| Affection (love and caring) | Helping other people | Privacy |
| Arts | Helping society | Public service |
| Challenging problems | Honesty | Purity |
| Change and variety | Independence | Quality of what I take part in |
| | | |
| Close relationships | Influencing others | Quality relationships |
| Community | Inner harmony | Recognition (respect from others, status) |
| Competence | Integrity | Religion |
| Competition | Intellectual status | Reputation |
| Cooperation | Involvement | Responsibility and accountability |
| Country | Job tranquility | Security |
| Creativity | Knowledge | Self-respect |
| Decisiveness | Leadership | Serenity |
| Democracy | Location | Sophistication |
| Ecological awareness | Loyalty | Stability |
| Economic security | Market position | Status |
| Effectiveness | Meaningful work | Supervising others |

| Efficiency | Merit | Time freedom |
|---|---|---|
| Ethical practice | Money | Truth |
| Excellence | Nature | Wealth |
| Excitement | being around people who are open and honest | Wisdom |
| Fame | Order (tranquility, stability, conformity) | Work under pressure |
| Fast living | Personal development | Work with others |
| Financial gain | Freedom | Working alone |

o   Once you have identified five values, write them down and post them in several prominent places around your home and office.

o   Whenever you need to chair a meeting, create or deliver a presentation, or conduct an important conversation, refer to your list and ask yourself if you are representing one or more of your values with your content and/or your style. By checking your list, you may realize that the entire communication you are about to give is so out of synch with your values that you may choose not to pursue or deliver it.

**Example:** I place a high value on creativity. At times I am offered the opportunity to teach courses or programs using a curriculum that is written by someone else. I have learned that if I do not have the flexibility to add my own creative touches to the material, it is better for me to turn the assignment down. It is next to impossible for me to be effective teaching from a curriculum that is not creative. Of course, we don't always have the luxury of turning down an assignment or a presentation and if I were forced to use material lacking in creativity, I would find ways to make the delivery of the presentation more creative.

There are many ways that you can insert your values into a communication. Sometimes it will be in the choice of material itself – the sources you cite, the words and examples you choose. Sometimes it's in the delivery – the way you dress, the tone of voice you use, the props and visuals you share. And sometimes you can insert your values by simply stating them – "I am passionate about …," "I feel strongly about …," or "_____ is very important to me." Asserting your values will give your presentation and communication more impact, which, in turn, will make it more powerful and effective. In acting parlance, a performer who has not done the work of infusing a performance with his or her special take on the material is said to be "phoning in" the performance. It's obvious when someone "phones in" a performance or any other type of communication. There is a lack of energy or sometimes there is an overabundance of unfocused energy. It can feel like a lot of form but no substance and can leave the listener feeling uninspired. However, by connecting your communication to a larger purpose and expressing and sharing an authentic part of yourself, you will have given something *valuable* to your listener and that's what true communication is all about. Remember: The consistency between how one appears and what one values is what helps turn an ordinary actor into a star – and an ordinary person into a superstar communicator.

Helping you find your "It" factor is difficult to do within the pages of a book. It's not always that much easier during a coaching session. However, I encourage you to spend some time uncovering it for yourself. Not only will it make your communication more engaging for your listeners, it will make each presentation you give easier and more enjoyable for you because it will be connected to something you really care about. And speaking of delivering presentations ... Lights ... Camera ... Action!

# PART III

# IT'S SHOWTIME!

## DEALING WITH STAGE FRIGHT!

We've all heard the statistics: for decades, people have ranked public speaking as their number one fear – many survey takers, ranking it more frightening than death. The fear of public speaking essentially comes from the fear of looking foolish and being exposed.

When people ask how they can get over their nerves, the first thing I tell them is that they probably can't get over their nerves and they shouldn't even try. What you need to do is to make friends with your nerves. You may be thinking, "Whoa! I respectfully disagree. My nerves are what make my knees shake, my palms sweat, my heart race, and my mouth go dry. They are not my friends! They are my enemies."

Think about what happens when you are in the presence of a person you really like and admire. Think about what it was (or is) like to be in the presence of someone you had a major crush on. Or think about the feelings that come over you when you are about to go on the biggest, baddest roller coaster in the amusement park.

What happens when you even anticipate these events? I'm sure for some of you, your knees shake, your palms sweat, your heart races, and your mouth goes dry. However, in these instances, those sensations could easily be attributed to excitement. The emotions of fear and excitement are often two sides of the same coin. We become nervous/excited around the person we are "crushing" on because we like them so much and we want them to like us back. We get nervous/excited about the roller coaster because even though we may scream through the entire ride we know how much fun it will be.

I invite you to reframe your "stage fright" by looking at it as excitement rather than nerves. Excitement is a positive emotion whereas nervousness is not. Consider being excited about doing your presentation because you like your audience so much that you want to share your information with them. You are excited about your presentation because, even though standing in front of all those people might be scary, you know how much fun it will be to share what you know. The reason most people have a hard time thinking of public speaking or giving presentations as an exciting activity is that so few of us are taught to focus on the right things while giving a presentation.

> *"I am convinced that we must train not*
> *only the head, but the heart and hand as well."*
> MADAME CHIANG KAI-SHEK

Studies prove overwhelmingly the importance of emotional engagement in communication, and research clearly concludes that communication is not about what you say but about how you say it and how it is perceived. Yet schools, businesses, and organizations continually lead us to believe that content is king. So from grade school on up we are taught that if we do our research and say (or in most cases, read) the right words, we have delivered an effective presentation. Therefore, most of the time when people stand in front of a room to present, they focus on their content. Am I going to remember my words? Did I do enough research? Are my listeners going to think I'm smart? I'm successful? I'm right? Fill in the blank. In addition, for some (okay most) of us, other questions race through our heads. Do I look fat? Is my hair okay? Do I have spinach in my teeth?

How many times has at least one of those thoughts creeped into your head before or during a presentation? With all those unanswerable questions running around in your head, no wonder you feel nervous instead of excited.

## How to Befriend Your Nerves

### Reset Your Camera Angle

I talked earlier about how the *close-up* helps a film audience get into the head of a character. We get to see the micro expressions and can infer what the actors are thinking, feeling, and saying. Then, at some point, the camera will switch angles and we get to see what the other person or persons in the scene are seeing or feeling.

Most of the time when you present, you have your internal camera angled for a close-up – of *yourself.* You are primarily focused on what you are doing, thinking, feeling, and saying. Remember all those questions that run around in your head? Am *I* going to remember my words? Did *I* do enough research? Are my listeners going to think *I'm* smart? *I'm* successful? *I'm* right? *Me, Me,* ME!

In order to turn nerves into excitement, I would like you to turn that camera around and have it focus on your audience. When you reset your camera angle, the questions running through your head should be: *What does my audience need to know? How can I best engage them so they can easily grasp what it is I want to share with them? Are they getting all the wonderful information I feel they need? Am I reaching them? Will they leave here more informed? Happier? Inspired?*

Notice how these questions differ from the questions that race through your mind when you are nervous.

**Bottom Line.** Focus more on what you have to give and less on the feedback (both negative and positive) you might get, and you will be less likely to feel nervous and more likely to feel excited. When 99% of your focus is on giving, you have much less time to worry about the fears your lizard brain is manufacturing.

## Two More Reasons to Befriend Your Nerves

1. **Being nervous gives you energy.** When you make friends with and accept your nerves instead of trying to suppress them, you can channel that nervousness into energy. This energy is an essential ingredient to delivering a powerful presentation. Many of us think that we can stand in front of a group of people and use the same energy we use for a one-on-one conversation. Although some presentations you see may seem conversational in tone, I guarantee that the speaker has amped up his/her energy level.

   My husband once met with the comedian Chris Rock on a business matter. Afterward he remarked about how un – Chris Rock he seemed. When asked during an interview why he seems so different in one-on-one conversations than he does onstage, Rock replied, "People don't pay to see me; they pay to see me; magnified by three." While most of us cannot get away with using the type of energy Chris Rock uses on stage, we should realize that our onstage energy needs to be magnified. Using the energy created by our nerves/ excitement will help us do that.

2. **Being nervous means you care.** I half joke with my clients that if they weren't nervous, I'd worry that they might be sociopaths. But it's true. The nerves/excitement you feel before you do a presentation signals that you care about the outcome. Caring is a good thing. We just need to

make sure we are caring about things that will be useful to us and beneficial for our listeners. If you did not feel any sensation about presenting in front of a large group, I would worry that you are not invested in or committed to what it is you are talking about and not invested in or committed to whether or not your listeners receive the information you are sharing.

I can tell you from firsthand experience that thinking you don't need to be excited or nervous is the kiss of death. I vividly remember two times when I went into a situation thinking I was hot stuff and knew my material so well that I had no need to do my usual extra level of mental or physical preparation before my presentation. Both times I realized once I hit the stage that I was missing something. Then, instead of being able to turn my nervous energy into excitement, I started experiencing all the negative sides of nervousness. I focused solely on me and started beating myself up for not having done more preparation. I started feeling like I looked unprepared which, of course, snowballed. Because I knew all too well the slippery slope I was headed down, I was able to reroute my trip and started focusing on my audience. However, although I *was* able to change course and reset my camera, I still think of those two presentations as my two least successful to date, and they probably were. I can still viscerally feel the discomfort I felt then. As I stated earlier, people's opinion about you is formed in the first seconds. If my first several seconds read uncomfortably, many of my audience members picked up on it. I will never strive to get rid of my nerves again.

**Q: But what about giving business presentations when I don't really feel invested?**

A: I understand there are times when you feel you have been asked to present on a topic that is intrinsically boring and of no interest to you. What can you do? I believe that whatever your topic, you can find something about it that is engaging. You can try to find an analogy or comparison for the material that makes it less boring. You can also use it as an opportunity to share any deeper or related insights you have that might elevate the material. A last resort is to acknowledge to your listeners that the material may seem a little dry or obtuse. Then share with your audience the "why" behind the need for that material to be presented.

Remember, every time you stand up at work or anywhere else to speak, you have an opportunity to make an impact on the people sitting in front of you. A positive, energized impact is going to be much more beneficial to you in the long run, so it's important to figure out a way to make your material interesting to you. When given a topic you might not have chosen for yourself, focus on how the information is going to enlighten, help, or inform the people you are sharing it with. Sometimes it might mean asking your boss, supervisor, or colleagues what they see as the bottom line. From there, work to identify the WIIFT and then create an engaging Teaser. By using the techniques I describe in this book, you should be able to turn a boring presentation into something that you can feel excited to share. I have worked with CPAs (to my mind, arguably the most boring profession of all) and have found a way for them to present their material in more engaging ways. If accounting can be engaging, then anything can be engaging.

## OTHER STAGE-FRIGHT-BUSTING TECHNIQUES

If you are thinking, "Reframing might help me think of my nervousness as excitement, but what about all those annoying physical sensations?" Here is a list of techniques to help mitigate the outward manifestations of your excitement.

### Tense and release

This technique is about creating the greatest amount of tension that you can in specific areas of your body and then releasing the tension to experience extreme relaxation, It's used in Yoga, for sleep disorders, and by many actors. It works and is fairly easy to do without looking too weird.

- Close your eyes. As tightly as possible. Contract all the muscles in your face. Hold for several seconds, then release.
- Then stretch open wide all of your facial muscles, hold, release.

- Continue tensing/contracting all of the muscles in your body, one section at a time ... arms, shoulders, hands, legs, buttocks. Hold for several seconds, then release.
- Tense your entire body, then release.

**Neck and shoulder rolls**

- Let your head drop gently forward. Roll it gently to the right, then to the left, return to center and repeat.
- Be gentle with your head and neck, especially when going to the back.

**Deep-Breathing/ Yogic breathing**

This is the same breathing you learned in the Vocal section. Purposefully going through deep-breathing exercises before the presentation will help to calm you.

- Breathe in deeply and slowly, filling your stomach first with air.
- Hold your breath for several seconds before you slowly release.
- Repeat, extending the amount of time you hold your breath.

**Running in place/ Jumping Jacks.**

Many people try to control nerves and wind up shutting down all emotion, turning themselves into speaking zombies. This happens when you are so determined not to look nervous that you become numb and wooden. If you are one of those people, physical exercise right before you walk into the room can be helpful. Go into the hallway or restroom and do a few jumping jacks or run in place. (Be sure to check your hair afterwards.)

**Act "as if"**

This can be a very powerful and effective technique. It's taken directly from the acting world, but many business people use it to great effect.

- Think of someone whose public speaking style you really admire. It could be a friend or colleague, a coach, or someone you see on television.
- Watch or imagine that person giving a speech or presentation. Pay careful attention to how they gesture, stand, move, smile, sound. Even notice how they take their breaths.
- Try on this person's persona. Try to match or mirror the gestures, stance, and other things that you noticed about this person. How does that feel? Now, close your eyes and imagine that person giving the presentation you are about to give.
- Next time you need to give a presentation and you are feeling less than confident, close your eyes and imagine yourself with all the positive presentation skills of

that other person. Then open your eyes and do your presentation as though you had all those skills that of other person.

As I spoke about in the "Looking the Part" section of this book, body language can not only affect the way people feel about you, it can affect the way you feel about yourself. So adopting another person's body language will help you to feel the confidence and/or power that the person you are emulating feels. Actors use this technique to "get into character." The more they take on physical aspects of a personality type, the easier it is to feel like that type. Don't think you have to be the next Marlon Brando to do this "right"; we instinctively and unconsciously match and mirror people all the time when we are talking to them.

**Try This:**

Walk into a room full of people and watch how often two people in conversation with each other have adopted the same or similar body language. Now consciously try to adopt another person's body language, breathing, and/or vocal tone. How do you feel different?

## Take up Space

This is a simple and scientifically supported way to gain confidence before entering into any situation. I mentioned earlier that by not covering your torso with crossed arms or by standing behind a podium, you appear more confident and engaging. However, there is now research, by psychologist and Harvard University Professor Amy Cuddy, which proves that by assuming an expanded, confident standing or seated position, you actually raise the level of testosterone in your body and lower the level of the stress hormone, cortisol, thus raising your confidence level and causing you to emanate that confidence.

**Try This:** Before your next meeting or presentation, go into the restroom or another private space and assume a Wonder Woman or Superman position, with legs wide apart, arms spread wide, and above your head. Hold the position for at least two minutes. Then go into your event with that additional hormonal boost.

**You can do this in a seated position too:**

Lean back in a chair in that "I'm the boss" posture. Legs into a figure four position, hands behind your head with elbows out. Stay in that position for two minutes. Caution: You will want to shift out of that position if you are going to be interviewing or communicating to a superior so that you do not come off as arrogant.

### Find a "Fan"

We hear a lot of crazy reports about celebrities being stalked by fans, but for the most part, celebrities and stars really cherish having a strong, vocal, and supportive fan base. Without fans, they don't sell out at the box office; they don't get magazine covers or TV appearances, which greatly affects their bottom line. As a star communicator, it's also helpful to rely on a little fan support. Nothing can ease your jitters faster than catching the eye of someone in your audience who is smiling and nodding during your speech or presentation. That friendly face can act as an anchor for you and give you added energy and confidence.

I was recently at a two-day conference and one of the speakers sat at my table the day before she was supposed to speak. We had a lot in common and really got along well. The day she was to present, I was sitting up front and genuinely smiled and nodded in response to the terrific job she was doing. It became clear to me that during the course of her speech she was using me as a fan anchor. She included the whole room of people in her presentation, using eye contact skills that I outlined in the earlier chapter, but whenever she needed an extra boost of energy, she knew I was there to provide it. After the presentation, just as I suspected, she told me how important it was for her to see "my smiling face" in the audience to come back to. I highly recommend you identify a "fan" in the audience who will make you feel comfortable. If you worry that there won't be anyone in your audience to fit the bill, you can always invite your own. If it's a formal presentation, see if you can bring along an assistant or colleague who will be sure to nod and smile just when needed. If it's a work meeting, try to make sure a supportive colleague is there, seated where you can easily make eye contact.

**BUT ... be careful NOT to get so comfortable with this friendly face that you deliver the majority of your content to them and neglect the rest of your audience, as we discussed in the "Eye Contact" section on page 131.**

### Visualization

This last technique for easing nerves can be extremely powerful and effective, though it is sometimes underated. Many athletes, professional musicians, and therapists swear by it. As a certified Neural Linguistic Programming (NLP) Practitioner, I know how powerful visualization is for overcoming fears and phobias. You can start using visualization from the moment you hear that you are going to be presenting something. Close your eyes and get quiet. Start to picture yourself giving a powerful, engaging, informative presentation. If you know what the space looks like, really try to picture yourself in the space. "See" yourself being confident, comfortable and composed. How are you standing? What are you wearing? How are you breathing? What are you hearing? What sensations are you feeling? What are you seeing? Imagine how you would like the audience to respond. See them nodding, clapping, smiling, listening – engaged.

An added step to this process would be for you to think back on a time in your life when you were feeling the confidence you would like to feel during your presentation. Where were you? What was going on? Then ask yourself all the above questions and as you recall that moment of feeling confident, try to feel the feelings you were feeling, see the things you were seeing. Mentally create a snapshot or a film clip of yourself that you can use when you think about the presentation you are about to give. Then on the day of your presentation, step into that snapshot or film clip and experience all of the confidence you imagined.

**Bottom Line:**

- Excitement and nervousness are two sides of the same coin
- Nerves prove that we care about doing a good job
- Nerves give presentations energy

# SET DESIGN

I made it clear in the beginning of this book how important the visual element of communication is to your overall message. However, the visual information being processed by your audience or listeners includes not just you, but also your environment and surroundings. This means that the items or scenery you have around you will impact people's perception of you and your presentation. Set designers in theatre and art directors for film put a lot of painstaking effort into finding the right props, colors, and locations to support the director's vision of the script.

In most cases you do not have the opportunity to transform your speaking environment. Some presenters like to invest in branded items, banners, posters, or table cloths that they can bring along to brighten up a dull space. The most important thing, however, is to make sure nothing in the space will distract from you and your presentation.

If you are going to be presenting at a new space, see if there is a way for you to see it ahead of time. If it's in another city, see if you can find photos of the space or ask your contact person for a general description. For a recent presentation I had to do, I neglected to practice what I preach. The whole time I was preparing for the workshop, I was picturing a classroom-type space with seats where the participants would be seated in front of me. When I got there, it was actually a smallish conference room where the participants were seated around a table. This didn't throw me off completely but it did distract me at first because it was so different from what I had envisioned.

If it is not possible or appropriate to see the space beforehand or to get a good description of it, be sure to show up early enough to have ample time to check the space out and make changes if necessary and if possible. Even if you are very familiar with the space, arriving at least a half an hour early is advised. You never know what could have happened in the space since the last time you were there.

**How to prepare your room:**

1) **Check your electronic equipment**

    This is a critical first step if you're using PowerPoint or anything else like it. You want to make sure the equipment is in the room and that it works properly. And always be prepared to go without your electronic media in the event of technical difficulties. Print out a hard copy of your slide presentation in case you need to go without the actual slide show.

2) **Move or remove the podium**

    If you show up for a presentation and there is a podium front and center, ask if you can move the podium to the side. As I mentioned in the section on posture, your torso is the most vulnerable part of your body and allows people to be more trusting of you. Standing behind a podium cuts off your torso and has an impact on how easily your audience can relate to you If you are one of several people presenting, try to get a feel for the stage and see how you can either stand to the side of, or in front of the podium.

If it is a very high stage, see what the sight lines are for the participants if you stand on the floor instead of on the stage. In a small room with a small audience, you may feel more connected to your audience and, vice versa, if you address them from the floor and not the raised stage.

For very large rooms, however, if there is a raised stage you should use it. It would be problematic *not* to. If you stand on the floor in front of a large audience, the people in the back rows may only be able to see your head because your torso will be hidden by the people sitting in the front rows.

**What if the mike is attached to the podium?**

That's an unfortunate situation for two reasons: a) You might have to stand behind the podium and b) Podium microphones are usually awful. First, ask if they have a lavaliere or a body mike. If they don't have one, see if you can remove the mike from the podium. If you can, I actually think it's better to hold a microphone than to stand behind a podium. However, if you'll need to use your hands to click your remote or hold notes, holding a microphone may not be advisable.

**If you find out that it's the podium or nothing:**

- Avoid the podium clutch – grabbing onto the sides of the podium and holding on for dear life.

- Avoid looking down at your papers the majority of the time. With your notes conveniently placed on the raised surface of the podium, it's more tempting to read directly from them. Don't!

- Stand on something if the top of the podium hits your collar bone or above. For people who are vertically challenged, it's advisable to ask for a step stool or some phone books to stand on so that more of your torso can be seen over the podium.

- Remember to gesture. Since much of your torso will be covered by the podium, be sure to bring extra energy to you presentation by using gestures.

**3) Make sure the area behind you is clear of distracting items.**

You don't want there to be pictures, posters, chairs, boxes, etc. that might take focus from you or your presentation.

**4) Check participant seating.**

You may need to adjust the seats in the audience to assure maximum comfort and participation. If you know the size of your audience, make sure to have just enough chairs (give or take a few) set up. Remove extra chairs if possible or put them off to the side. This will discourage people from sitting in orphan seats and it will avoid the feeling of speaking to a sparsely occupied room.

## PROPS

There are many props you may need to bring or have available during a presentation or speech. Some props are necessary for the smooth facilitation of the presentation while others add a little spice and sparkle. Here is my short list of both types:

**Flip Chart with Markers.** Always ask the host if these will be provided. I've invested in a portable pad which, depending on the venue, I will bring with me. Even though you may be using PowerPoint, there are often things that you need to write down: questions from the audience, what they want to get out of the presentation, illustrations. Having different visual references keeps the participants' brains active.

**Hand-held remote to advance your slides.** Many places will provide this but some don't. Buying your own wireless remote is the best option. It comes with a small device that plugs into a USB port and works with any computer.

And yes, it's important to use a remote. This prevents you from hiding behind your computer and frees you to walk around the room.

And *do* check your batteries before you leave your home or office and bring extras. Twice I've forgotten to do this and it caused me unnecessary frustration.

**Handouts** – Workbooks and handouts can be great ways to bolster and support your presentation. However, they can also be great at distracting people from listening to your presentation. You need to be very careful about how and when you use handouts. If it is a short presentation (one hour or less), unless the written material is *critical* for the participants to have, I would not hand it out until the end of the presentation. If it is a worksheet, I would suggest handing it out shortly before it is needed. Why? Because otherwise, the handout can easily become the focal point and instead of having all eyes on you, you have all eyes on your handout. It is very difficult to speak to the bent heads of audience members.

For a longer presentation or workshop, you may need to hand out the workbooks. I make my PowerPoint and my delivery close to the workshop material, and interesting. That way, participants only look at the handouts when there is a specific need to do so.

**PowerPoint** – So much controversy over a single inanimate piece of software! Voices holler for the end of PowerPoint, claiming that it kills presentations. PowerPoint has been held responsible for millions of boring presentations being conducted in boardrooms across the country. PowerPoint doesn't kill presentations, people kill presentations. Blaming the slides for a boring presentation is like blaming the dining room for a boring dinner party.

I used to be the first one on the anti-PowerPoint bandwagon but I've since realized that it can be a very effective tool when wielded by responsible presenters with engaging delivery skills. People remember **45%** more of your presentation when you support it with visual aids, and PowerPoint or one of its equivalents is a highly effective visual support.

## TIPS FOR USING POWERPOINT EFFECTIVELY:

PowerPoint is blamed for creating snoozefests because of two main abuses presenters commit:

1) Cramming too much information on each slide.
2) Proceeding to face the screen and reading all that information from the slide.

Both abuses can be remedied.

The most important two things to remember about creating PowerPoint slides are **Simplicity** and **Clarity**. Less is more. The information on the slides should be in outline form. Slides are best used to support what you are saying and to add information that you may, by choice or by accident, leave out of your presentation. Ultimately, you want eyes on you the majority of the time. The audience should be watching the slides only if they get confused, want clarification, or when a picture speaks louder than words.

Below are some general guidelines for using PowerPoint with your presentation. None of them are etched in stone.

- Use one main point in each slide with no more than 5-6 lines of text and 7 – 10 words per line.
- Use one visual per two minutes of presenting. Again, not etched in stone, but this is a good rule of thumb for measuring how many slides you need based on the length of your presentation. An hour-long presentation should have less than 30 slides.
- Use phrases, *not* full sentences – eliminate articles, conjunctions, and adjectives wherever possible. The only complete sentences should be quotations.
- Use bullets, numbers, and clear, consistent typeface . Using color is great, but no more than three or four colors, and make sure the colors are not distracting.
- Make each phrase short and relevant – think newspaper headlines. Make sure information has a direct relationship with your bottom line and/or the plot point you are discussing.
- Practice – Set up, Put up and Shut up: **Set Up** – prepare your listeners by talking about the slide you are about to show; **Put Up** – show the slide. **Shut Up** – pause long enough for your listeners to take in the information on the slide.
- You don't need to read everything on the slide. This is something that most people don't realize. With very technical and data-heavy presentations, you may want

to make the audience aware of many important facts. However, you don't have to read each point. Choose the most important and the most interesting facts to read or highlight and let your audience read the rest to themselves if they so choose.

## Bottom line: Dos and Don'ts for using PowerPoint

- DO face the audience, not the board or screen. It's difficult to resist reading along with your slides, but *resist* it. You don't want your audience to spend the presentation watching just one side of your face.
- DO Make sure visuals and typeface is large enough to be seen by everyone
- DO have lots of white space
- DO use charts, graphs, and pictures
- DO use slides to highlight key points, long statistics, and quotes
- DON'T READ your slide – you can glance at it occasionally or have a computer in front of you to refer, to or use notes.
- DON'T present a slide until you are ready to talk about it
- DON'T leave the same slide up too long
- DON'T use too many different typefaces and make sure the typeface you choose is easy to read.
- DON'T stand in front of your slides – Stand to the left or right of them. If you see light in your eyes from the projector - move.

**Other Visual Aids** – sample of a product or an item that illustrates a point in your presentation.

I once worked with a client who was representing a very high-end alcoholic beverage. This client loved to use props in his presentations. One of the props he loved to use was a New Year's Eve – type popper – the kind that explodes and spouts confetti. In the middle of the presentation he brought out the popper, popped it, and confetti flew about the audience. He felt that this woke people up and illustrated the excitement of the product. Though I'm big on adding excitement and all about using visuals to illustrate a point, the popper was one of the first things I recommended he get rid of. First of all, he was representing a very expensive, very classy brand, and the popper seemed cheap and cheesy – very incongruent. Since he loved props so much, I suggested that when he explained how his product is made, he use the analogy of a lump of coal turning into a diamond; he could then use coal pieces and diamonds as props. These images are much more consistent with his brand and his message.

**Music** – I like to use music during my presentations whenever it's possible and appropriate. I use it before the session begins, during the break, and during certain breakout group or partner exercises. The music choice and use depends on the group and the location. I will choose a high-energy, well-known song to play before I deliver a more inspirational or motivational presentation, but a more mellow song before a training or workshop. I usually choose instrumental, mellow tunes during breakout sessions and more energetic songs during the breaks.

## SET DESIGN AND PROPS FOR MEETINGS

If you are having a meeting in your office or in your company's conference room, the setting and props are still going to be important. Any disorder or messiness will have an impact on the person you are meeting with. This goes for the quality of your props as well.

If you are using a conference room, it's a good idea to set it up the way you would like it, before the meeting. Place whatever materials you' want to share with the client or prospect in front of the chair or chairs you would like them to sit in. This will avoid the awkward moment of entering the room and not knowing where everyone should sit. For over ten years I've been a consultant with a company that does training for financial advisors. I role play different prospects or clients and take meetings with the financial advisor, giving my honest feedback afterwards. Walking into a meeting and seeing scattered or messy material on the desk is an immediate red flag. If the person cannot be organized with his materials for a meeting, how organized will he be with my important documents and my money?

So the next time you're preparing to hold a meeting, don't forget to design your set and check your props.

## Handling Questions and Answers

Once the main portion of the meeting, presentation, or speech is over, most listeners assume they will be able to ask you questions.

A good idea is to state at the beginning of your presentation, how you will deal with questions. If you are very confident that you can answer questions without getting sidetracked or thrown off, then choose times in your presentation to ask if anyone has questions, or state towards the beginning of your presentation that if anyone has any questions they should feel free to ask.

However, if you have a lot of material and are not confident that you will be able to get through it if you answer too many questions, tell people in your introduction that you will leave time at the *end* of the presentation for questions. Of course, because people quickly forget things, some may raise their hands in the middle of your speech, anyway. If that happens, it's okay to remind them by saying, "I have so much to share/cover. I'd love it if you could hold your question till the end." Still, when some people really feel they have a burning question, it might be best to take a moment to listen. If you can't answer briefly, tell them that you will definitely get back to them, or that you will answer within the presentation.

*Points to remember when taking questions:*

- Look at the person who is talking and acknowledge what they are saying verbally or nonverbally. Seems like a no-brainer, but

Whiz Kids often neglect to do this and answer the question as if it has appeared from the stratosphere.

- Repeat the question or paraphrase the question. This is a very important point for three reasons:

1) It shows the questioner that you have heard them and also gives them an opportunity to correct anything that you may have misunderstood about their question. How many times have you asked a question and had the person you ask launch into a long-winded answer for a completely different question? Repeating or paraphrasing the question saves you time and the embarrassment of answering the wrong question.

2) Repeating the question allows the rest of the audience who may not be sitting near the questioner to hear the question. This is a real pet peeve of mine. I have been in too many audiences where the speakers take questions and start giving answers while 80% of the audience hasn't even heard the question. That being said, it's also a very easy thing to forget to do, so try to ingrain it into your thinking. As much as I hate being on the audience end of this omission, I must confess I've been guilty myself of not repeating some questions from the stage.

3) It can give you needed time to think of an answer. Very helpful in interview situations. As you put the question into your own words, your brain has an opportunity to come up with an answer for it.

- **Look at the entire audience when answering one person's question.** Some people actually suggest that in a large audience, you move away from the person who has asked the question so that you are physically including everyone when you begin to answer. The reason behind this theory is that there is a danger of losing the attention of other audience members if in answering one person's question you turn it into a one-on-one dialogue. This is also true during smaller meetings or for group interviews. Always realize that if one person has that question, chances are someone else may have the same question, so include the rest of the listeners when answering.

- **Make answers short and direct.** Even though you want to treat the answer like you are addressing the whole audience, you don't want to make the answer another speech. Giving too long an answer usually has the effect of either sounding defensive or overstating your case. In front-of-the-room presentations it will also make the rest of the audience restless because they have just sat through a full presentation and are ready for things to start winding down. They also may have questions of their own and fear that you will now not have time for them.

- **If you don't know the answer, say so.** Fudging or making things up when you don't know the answer will more than likely backfire. First of all, your nonverbals will most likely give you away by causing you to breathe differently, stutter, perspire, or blush. And secondly, even if you have a great poker face, if you make something up and someone in the audience or at the meeting or interview knows the truth and corrects you, your credibility is shot.

No matter how much of an expert you are or how high a position you have, you cannot know everything. There's a great saying that goes something like, "You don't have to be the library, just the librarian." If you don't know the answer, tell the person that you will do what you can to find out the answer and get back to them. In certain presentations this is a great opportunity to ask the questioner for their contact information and to stay in touch.

- **Check in.** Once you've given your answer, it's a great idea to ask: "Does that answer your question?" or "Have I answered your question?" This will help to clarify if you "got" their question, especially if you've forgotten to paraphrase it when they ask.

- **Use encouraging body language.** Make sure body language encourages and does not discourage questions. If you say that you're open for questions and then begin gathering your papers and materials or stand or sit with your eyes averted and your arms crossed, you are sending mixed messages.

- **Don't allow one person to dominate.** If one person asks long and continuous questions, it's okay to tell them: "I would love to spend more time answering your question, but I'm concerned that there isn't enough time or that other people may have questions."

## DEALING WITH DIFFICULT QUESTIONS:

Many of the questions you get after an informative presentation will be asking for further information or for clarification. However, during meetings, interviews, or persuasive and sales presentations, you may get emotionally fueled questions that want to challenge, discredit, or provoke you. The first thing you want to know about emotionally fueled questions is that they are usually based on some type of fear. So before you answer:

- **Listen for the question under the question:** What do they really want to know? People will often ask a question that is not addressing their real concern but is masking a fear. Try to understand the fear that is behind a difficult question and address the fear if you can.

  For example: Often when people ask about price or safety, they are really worried that it is not worth the price, that they can't afford the price, that it doesn't do what you say it does ,etc., etc. When answering questions of this type, answer in a way that will address and calm those fears.

- **Acknowledge the emotions:** When someone is extremely emotional, acknowledge their concerns before you answer the question. "*It sounds like you're concerned/upset/confused/ angry ... because ...,*" OR, "*I can understand you feel ...,*" THEN attempt to answer their concerns/questions

- **Learn to bridge:** I spoke about bridging earlier in this book but if you missed it, it's worth repeating. When you are faced with a difficult topic that you do not wish to get deeply into, or that you are not prepared to go into, answer the question as honestly and as briefly as possible, then bridge to a topic that you feel more comfortable and informed about.

    o   Take 10 seconds to answer the question or address the concern.
    o   Take five second to bridge to something you want to discuss or are more prepared to talk about.
    o   Spend 30 seconds talking about the topic you feel more comfortable talking about.

This is a very important technique and can be used effectively in job interviews as well. When the interviewer asks you about an experience or a quality that you are not particularly confident speaking about, spend a few seconds on that topic and then bridge to talking about one of your strengths and how it matches with the firm's needs.

# BLOOPERS! AND HOW
# TO HANDLE THEM

Many movies and TV shows have started including blooper reels at the end of the "polished" productions. Blooper reels are fun ways of saying even movie stars make mistakes. Audiences get a good laugh over seeing the stars' blooper reels and the stars enjoy laughing at themselves. So why is it that in "real life" communication, most of us feel there is absolutely no margin for error. Let's talk about how we can deal with some of the most common communication bloopers.

**What if I forget my lines?**

This is a fear voiced by many of my clients: *I'm afraid I'm going to go blank and then what?* Or, *I'm afraid I'm going to say the wrong thing or say something stupid.* And someone asked me via Twitter: *"What do you do when the words won't come to you? I constantly find myself searching for the simplest term. Help, Mommy brain!"*

When you're in the middle of a conversation with a friend and you make a mistake or lose your train of thought, you probably stop and correct yourself, laugh, and start again; you might joke that you're having a blond or senior moment or even mommy brain. But in other situations we expect ourselves to be perfect.

Think of your presentation as an elevated conversation between youself and other people. If you make a mistake or forget where you are, employ the same techniques as you would in a conversation with a friend. If you go blank, admit it. Pause and wait for your thought to come to you. If it doesn't come, move on. Tell your audience you've lost your train of thought and you're sure it will come back to you. Depending on your ActorType: You can make a joke and laugh about it (Innocent, Sex Symbol, Comic, Hero, Buddy). Or you can treat it as a slight annoyance but still make light of it. (Curmudgeon, SuperHero, Villain, Whiz Kid). If you forget a whole section or plot point, say so and go back and address it, or ask yourself if the information you forgot was really important. Maybe you can leave it out.

What most people do when they make a mistake during a presentation is take out a whip and begin using it on themselves. Beating yourself up is a sure way to derail your communication. Your listeners will be able to see that you have disengaged from them and will start to feel your discomfort without knowing why. Admitting your blooper, on the other hand, can create a bond between you and your listeners, just as watching movie stars mess up makes us feel that stars are a little more like us.

**What if nobody responds to my questions?**

What happens if you create a killer Teaser using "How many of you" questions, or you want to involve your audience by asking an open-ended question in the body of your presentation – and nobody raises a hand or calls out an answer? This is very rare, but you do want to be prepared in the event it happens.

**If no hands go up for HMOY question:**

Be prepared with a comeback. For example, if you ask, "How many of you are using the Superwidget?" No hands go up. Comeback: "Well, looks like we need to do a better job at marketing." Then: "How many of you would like to learn how to use the Superwidget?" No hands. Comeback: "I know once you find out how it can save you time, money, and space, all the hands in the room will be up." *and/or,* "Okay, how many of you just don't like raising your hand?" By making light of the lack of response, you show that you are confident about what you have to share and therefore are not worried about whether their hands go up or not. Audiences sometimes take a while to warm up (more on that below), so do not take this personally and do not chastise your audience (unless, of course, you are a Villain or Curmudgeon ActorType).

**If no response to Open Ended questions:**

**Turn it into a rhetorical question.** (Good for Innocents, Sex Symbols, and Whiz Kids) Be ready to answer the question yourself without skipping a beat. For example, you ask, "Who remembers one of the three elements of effective communication," and no hands go up. After a significant beat you give the answer: "There's the Vocal, Verbal ..." Taking that approach makes it seem like you know they wanted to answer but might be too shy or unsure of the answer, so you are going to help them out. Know that even if they do not verbally answer, once you ask the question, their brains are either forming the answer or searching for the answer and that mental activity has the effect of keeping them more engaged.

**Use the Army method of volunteering** (Great for Villains, Curmudgeons, Heroes, and Super Heroes) Scan your audience for someone who looks open, friendly, and engaged. Look for someone making eye contact with you, who maybe has nodded once or twice and looks interested. Then call on him or her by either saying, "You look like you're dying to answer," or, "What do you think? Take a guess. I promise this won't be graded" Sometimes by just making direct eye-contact with someone and smiling, you will convey the message that you would like them to answer and they will "volunteer."

*INCREASE YOUR ODDS OF GETTING ANSWERS BY:*

- **Making sure your question isn't too long and that you state it clearly.** When your question gets too wordy, it becomes hard to follow and people get insecure about answering because they're not sure that they understand what you're asking. Same, of course, goes for when they actually can't understand what you're asking because you drop energy at the end of the sentence, speak too fast, don't enunciate, or don't use enough volume.

- **Making sure you give people enough time to answer.** I see speakers ask a question and a second later move on before they get an answer. Audience members can be shy and will sometimes wait till one person takes the initiative to interact first. If you don't have a couple of bold people in the audience, response can be slow. Even for chatty audience members, it can take up to three or four seconds before they will answer. I know on stage that feels like an eternity, but it's not. Stand in an open position, smile, and wait. After enough time has gone by and no one has responded, use one of the above techniques.

- **Using open body language.** If you ask a question and then fold your arms across you chest or start flipping through your notes, you're sending the message that you really aren't interested in or have time for their answer. And don't forget to raise your hand first for "Show of Hands" questions. People will usually have a knee-jerk reaction and mirror you.

**What if someone hijacks my presentation with a long-winded and/or off-topic question or answer?**

Asking open-ended questions and taking questions does open up the possibility for you to lose control of your presentation. Some people will use this as an opportunity to state their opinions or give mini-presentations of their own.

**What to do:** Start by physically breaking rapport with the speaker – change your body position so that it's less open to him/her – and listen for one word that you can use to bridge back to your topic.

Do not be afraid to grab onto that word and run with it even if the person is in mid-sentence. If that technique doesn't work or if there is no way for you to bridge from their hijacking to your topic: use a strong diaphragmatic voice to state, say: "I appreciate your input and in the interest of time I really need to move on." Then physically move away from them and continue with your presentation.

If someone asks an unrelated or inappropriate question, you can politely tell them that this particular presentation is not dealing with that topic. Or say, "That's an interesting question and I'd love to answer it, but it's going to take us away from the main topic of my presentation, so in the interest of time, I'm going to have to speak to you afterwards."

**What if someone heckles me or talks during my presentation?**

Yes, it can happen. I've been fortunate enough to not have it happen to me (unless, of course, you count trying to teach public speaking to ninth graders!). Hecklers are like bullies. They need attention and will go to great lengths to get it, positive or negative. So you don't want to necessarily engage a heckler. And you don't want to ignore or look threatened by them. There are two methods you can use: Move as close as you can to where they are sitting and make eye contact with them as you continue to deliver your presentation. This alone may have the effect of quieting them or of having their friends quiet them. If that does not work, then in a calm voice say something like: "It sounds like you have quite a bit to say. Would you mind taking your conversation outside; I feel it's distracting for the rest of us." Or, "Excuse me. You're entitled to your opinion, and I'd appreciate it if you expressed it after my presentation. Right now there's a lot of information I'd like to share with the rest of the people here."

If the rest of the audience is engaged and involved in your presentation and you address the heckler in a pleasant yet assertive way, even if the offending person refuses to quiet down, usually someone in the audience or an event coordinator will come to your aid. If, for whatever reason, this does not happen, I suggest you stop your presentation and say something like, "I have a lot more information to share and I would love to share it with all of you; however, under these circumstances I don't think I can go on." If this does not quiet the heckler, cause an event organizer to step in, or if no audience member puts pressure on your doer to fly right, I would stay true to my word and start packing up. Your job is to give your audience information that will help them and possibly effect change in their lives. It's not possible to do this if you are being disrupted so much that it is distracting you and the rest of the audience.

Fortunately, this is not a common occurrence, but if it does happen you want to be pleasant and *assertive* – not submissive or aggressive – when dealing with these types of situations.

**My Motto:**

If you don't address the elephant in the room, you'll end up with a herd of elephants that will destroy your communication.

## FREQUENTLY ASKED QUESTIONS:

While I was writing this book, I posted a Twitter question asking people to tweet questions they would love me to answer. Many of these I've covered in the body of the text and in the section above. Below are specific answers to some of the other great questions tweeted to me, and other questions that I often hear from clients.

**Should you be very rehearsed, or learn to go "off the cuff"?**

The answer depends on your ActorType, your experience, and the event. Broadway plays have several months to rehearse, whereas most movies allow their actors mere days of rehearsals. The Broadway show involves a lot more moving pieces and does not allow you to cut and start again, so more time is needed to work out the kinks. Similarly, if you are doing a front-of-the-room presentation for a very large audience of people whom you do not know and whom you need to impress, you definitely want to plan it out, create an outline, practice, and possibly work with a coach. But being very rehearsed can backfire. Being over-rehearsed tends to make you stiff and unengaging because you get used to using a certain rhythm, pausing or not pausing at a certain place, stressing a certain word. Then when it is time to deliver the speech in front of people, your concentration is not on them, but on how you rehearsed the speech.

Which is why one thing you *never* want to do is to memorize a presentation. Memorizing your presentation is the kiss of death. But, you might say, actors have to memorize lines, don't they? Learning how to memorize a line and make it your own without it sounding canned or memorized is one of the key factors that separates good actors from bad ones. Some directors and acting teachers will go to great lengths to keep an actor from getting too set or comfortable in rehearsed roles. In fact, film directors have been known to instruct actors to do or say something completely unexpected during a scene with another actor just to get an honest unrehearsed reaction. Since most presenters are not highly trained actors and have not learned how to memorize and make the words still sound fresh, I strongly caution you not to memorize.

Aside from the fact that memorized presentations usually sound like R2-D2 when they are delivered, memorizing your "script" sets you up for other disasters. No matter how good a memory you have and no matter how long you have to memorize, once you are in front of an audience and nerves and distractions take over, you are likely to forget something. Once you forget just one word of a completely memorized speech, panic can set in and your whole presentation gets derailed.

In almost 20 years of teaching and training, I have *never* seen anyone successfully deliver a memorized speech. I tell all of my clients and students not to do it and there are always people who think they can get away with it.

I can tell within three minutes when a person is delivering a memorized speech. The vocal tone is flat or repeats the same predictable rhythm. One of the biggest telltale signs is the eyes. The eyes are constantly going to the upper-right position as the person tries to visually recall the written text. This makes you much less engaging because you are not in the present moment but are in the past trying to recall what you had written.

Another giveaway for a memorized speech is word choice. When you write out an entire speech, you tend to use different language than you would if you were to speak the speech. So the written and memorized presentation sounds canned and overly formal – "phoned in."

In some cases, a formal, flowery, or literary speech may be appropriate: eulogies, testimonials, and formal introductions are some examples. In those cases, I still advise against relying solely on your memory. In situations where you need to have your speech written out, you should get very comfortable with it and have the text written out on large index cards. Practice until you are comfortable reading a few words of a sentence, quickly memorizing the rest of the words in the sentence and then speaking those words while looking off the page and at your audience. This is a learned skill that can be worked on and mastered.

When I was acting, I took a class specifically in the skill of reading off the page. It's called cold-reading technique. For certain auditions actors are given the script just a day or two before, sometimes on the day of. There is not always enough time for you to memorize it, and even if you do memorize it, you will fall into the same traps that speakers do. Forgetting one line or word in a line will send you into panic mode and you could blow the whole audition. Learning this type of cold-reading – where you can read and still stay connected to your audience through eye contact – is essential.

If you have to give a less-formal presentation to a smaller group, or on topics that you feel very comfortable speaking about and speak about often, it's sometimes preferable to be, or at least to seem, more "off the cuff." But even off-the-cuff presentations should be thought out, outlined, and practiced. It's helpful to create a mind map or an outline of key words and phrases that touch on what you want to cover. Then spend time mentally and/or verbally using that outline to create several versions of your presentation, making sure that you don't get married to one way of presenting it. You'll be less likely to get stuck on one way of presenting it if you refrain from writing full sentences. It's okay to write out a full sentence for your Teaser, and maybe some of your transitions, but everything else should be written down as words or phrases.

*"The Academy urges winners not to read speeches, knowing that it's bad television. (And really, should any Oscar – winning actor claim not to be able to remember lines?) It's my firm belief that what comes out in the moment – or doesn't – is a true reflection of feeling,*

*whether the speech feels rehearsed and polished or immediate and spazzy."* – NATHANIEL ROGERS AND NATALIE MATTHEWS – RAMO. SLATE.COM, FEBRUARY. 24, 2012

### How about those *real* "off the cuff" situations?

You're in a big meeting and suddenly your manager turns to you and says, "Tell us what you think about X." Do you go into panic mode and draw a complete blank? We've all seen those improvisational shows where someone gives a bunch of actors a situation or character or a single word and they create a fleshed-out scene within minutes. This is not a skill that comes easily to everyone. Actors train for years to be good at improv. As speakers, you can train to be good at impromptu and off-the-cuff speaking as well. The "prompt" that you need to keep in mind is your bottom line or your Theme – the one thing you want people to remember. Everything you speak about should somehow lead back to and support that bottom line.

You can train yourself in this skill by choosing a topic and setting a timer for five minutes. In those five minutes think of as many specific emotional and logical examples that support that one topic as you can. Then set your timer again and tape yourself talking about that topic. Cut your preparation time down to four, then three, then two minutes. The more you practice this skill the more prepared you will be for the situation described above. So that the next time you're asked what you think about X, you will: Breathe. Pause. (Remember you don't always have to answer a question right away.) Take a moment to consider the main point you want to convey about X and choose one or two logical and emotional details to support that opinion – then shine forth with your words of wisdom.

**Is it okay to use notes?**

See the answer above on whether to be very prepared or off the cuff. But my general opinion is that it is better to use notes and check them occasionally, than to memorize and sound stiff and wooden – *as long as* the notes are just notes and not a completely written-out presentation.

**Notes about notes:**

- I recommend having notes written on 3x5 or 5x8 index cards and not on an 8x10 pieces of paper (it's okay to use an 8X10 sheet of paper folded in half). Why? When you use a full sheet of paper, the paper looks flimsy and messy as it flops, bends, or shakes in your nervous grip. Full sheets also invariably end up hiding your mouth when you hold them up to read – and if we can't see your mouth, we will have a hard time hearing you and paying attention.
- Make sure the notes you have written are large enough and clear enough for you to read and that there is a space between each line. This will keep you from squinting and getting lost when you look down to refer to them. I have experienced far

too many of my students and other speakers looking down at their notes as if the notes have suddenly turned into a foreign language that they can't understand. When I need to use notes during a presentation, I type them out, double-space them, and increase the font to 14 or 16 points. I will also sometimes highlight certain focus words so that when I look down, a particular word will stand out and remind me of the gist of my thought or idea.

- If there are more than one card or page of notes, be sure to number them. If your cards fall or get out of order, it could take forever for you to find your place. But be aware of having too many cards and making the audience fear that your presentation will never end.

I was leading a training once and one of the participants had a stack of 3x5 cards which she proceeded to read through. It was a large stack and she made the mistake of placing each card on the podium nearby when she had finished reading from it. I could feel the audience's (and my) anxiety mount, since it seemed that no matter how many cards she put down, a huge number of cards remained in her hand. Our attention then became focused on when and if her card stack was ever going to end. If she had put each card back in the stack, we would not have been made so aware of how large the stack was.

**What are some effective ways or tips to keep presentations to allotted time restrictions?**

Timing is always a challenge and one that I have personally struggled with. There are ways you can try to plan in advance how long certain material will take. The PowerPoint rule of thumb is two minutes per slide. Which means if you have an hour-long presentation, you should have no more that 25 – 30 slides. This doesn't mean that you rigidly spend two minutes on each slide. Some may take longer and some may take a lot shorter. However, it is a pretty accurate measure, providing you follow my guidelines of not putting too much information on each slide.

If you are not using PowerPoint, you can apply a similar formula by estimating that each outlined 8x10 page should take you about 5 – 10 minutes to get through.

It's also helpful to think about your presentation in separate sections that connect to your bottom line and decide what percentage of your allotted time will be spent on each section. Then divide each larger section into sections and decide how much time you would like to spend on each of these subsections. Sectioning off your presentation will also help because if your time is cut in any way, you will be able to choose which sections you can leave out. Many factors can impact the timing of your presentation. Factors like technical difficulties, late starts, and poor event planning can affect the allotted time you have.

I once worked on a presentation with a client that was supposed to be a 45-minute-long speech about a specific type of tax law. At the conference where she was to present, because of a series of unforeseen events, her presentation time was cut to 10 minutes! Because we were so clear in building the presentation in sections and having each of those sections closely tied to a bottom line, she was able to deliver the most important sections and the most important parts of those sections and get her main point across.

One of my clients calls his different sections "chunks." We have created several different chunks detailing different aspects of his overall bottom line. For each given situation he finds himself in – media interview, sales pitch, or stand-up presentation – based on the audience and the time constraints, he can choose which chunks to use, which chunk to lead with, and which chunks to leave out.

Even if you are given all the time allotted, keeping your presentation on track can be a challenge. For one thing, it is very hard to know in advance how interactive a group may turn out to be. An interactive group is a wonderful thing but it can really mess up your timing if you're not careful. That's why in this new world of computer applications, I've started employing different tools and strategies to keep me on track for presentations with a tight time schedules. I use a large timer that I downloaded onto my iPad. I then set the timer for the time I would like to spend on each section of my presentation. I have the timer count up or down and keep it facing me so that I can glance at it and know how much time has gone by or how much time is left. If I have an assistant with me, I have her show me the timer periodically so I know where I am. Of course, you can do the same thing if there is a clock in clear view.

**How do you sustain your audience's attention?**

I received quite a few questions on this topic. I believe one of the surest ways to keep an audience involved is to make sure you fully engage them in the very beginning with your Teaser/ attention getter and that you have illustrated clearly what is in it for them. However, sometimes people's attention may still drift even though you've started off with excellent engagement techniques. I appreciate that so many people on Twitter asked me about keeping and sustaining audience attention. I've seen too many presenters ramble on without seeming to care if their audience is involved or not.

I do want to point out that although it's important to notice and make adjustments when you see people's attention wander, you don't want to make yourself crazy if you notice one or two people who appear not to be involved. I know what it's like to focus on the one guy in the corner who keeps looking at his watch, feeling like your whole presentation is tanking. By the way, I have had several experiences where I was sure an individual was totally uninterested and unimpressed with my presentation, only to have that individual come up to me afterwards to tell me how much he or she enjoyed it. However, when more than a few individuals look disengaged, this may be a clue to use a technique to bring them back. I've addressed engaging the audience pretty thoroughly in the "Improving the Second Act – How to Keep Your Audience Engaged" section of this book. But for those of you who are reading this section out of order, here's a list of the techniques. You can go back to Chapter 18 for more detail.

- Ask questions
- Ask for volunteers
- Ask for a show of hands
- Encourage state changes
- Set up partner or group shares
- Use humor

That's it for the questions I am asked most often. I'm sure by now you may have come up with some of your own. If so feel free to drop me an e-mail, send me a tweet, or find me on Facebook. I will be sure to give you a detailed answer if I can.

I hope it's clear to you after reading this book how passionate and committed I am to raising the level of face-to-face communication. If you remember nothing else from this book, I hope you will remember these few things:

- Use your ActorType(s) to help you highlight your strengths and work on and downplay your weakness.
- Polish your nonverbal skills – your body language, gestures, and vocal tone – to make your communication shine.

- Organize your verbal skills so that your listeners know what's in it for them and what is the one thing you want them to remember.
- Discover your value and what you value most; confidently share both values with your listeners.
- Talk is Cheap, Communication is Priceless ... Don't just mouth words; connect and give something of value to your listeners.
- Finally, get out there and *speak*. We all have something important to share. Don't hide what you have to share under a bushel.

# A STAR IS BORN – EPILOGUE

Most movies last just about two hours and you can leave if you don't like what you are experiencing. The movie of our lives lasts a lot longer and as actor, writer, producer, and director, we get to design, rewrite, edit, and create sequels to it.

Growing up as background player in the movie of my life, I may have missed out on a few things. But it made me acutely aware of the importance of effective, authentic, congruent face-to-face communication. It has taken me many years to discover, experiment with, and hone the techniques I've outlined in this book.

I hope that in reading this book and putting some of these techniques into practice, you will gain the knowledge, confidence, and skills to help you speak and shine and become a sought-after box office draw in all your future endeavors. Now, go practice!

*"We are what we repeatedly do.*
*Excellence, then, is not an act, but a habit."*
—*ARISTOTLE*

# APPENDIX

I am privileged to know many extremely talented fashion stylists, designers, image consultants and personal branding experts. If after reading this book you feel you would like some expert advice in any of these areas, please go to my website where you will find an updated list of people and businesses I recommend.

www.speaketc.com/standing-ovation-presentations/